MICHAEL BORDEN

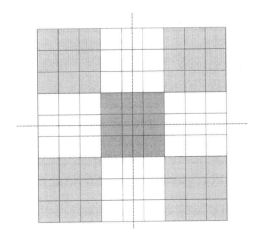

VASTU
ARCHITECTURE

DESIGN THEORY AND APPLICATION FOR EVERYDAY LIFE

Dedication

I dedicate this work to my teacher Dr. V. Ganapati Sthapati, whose tireless dedication to Vastu science has cultivated a renaissance of sacred architecture in the world today.

ISBN: 1456491784
ISBN-13: 9781456491789
Library of Congress Control Number: 2010919370

Table of Contents

Preface

The purpose of this book is to outline simply and clearly the technological and philosophical principles of Vastu science as applied to buildings for secular functions: houses, offices, libraries, hospitals, etc. I want to encourage the reader to cultivate a desire, through understanding, to create a Vastu structure for their home or office.

My motivation for this comes from the simple personal experience of seeing my life and the lives of my clients benefit from creating a relationship with Vastu knowledge and space. I believe Vastu science gifts us with a technology to create buildings with the *regenerative* properties of peace, prosperity, and love. Having the possibility of regeneration in a building is not a new concept. We all experience the regenerative effect of coming home to our special living space. Vastu science gives us an opportunity to further deepen the experience of regeneration.

As simple as it may seem to the reader, the application of Vastu principles often presents a challenge to the most experienced Vastu designer. The notion of taking the principles of this exact science and applying them to a modern structure, with all the programmatic idiosyncrasies of a modern lifestyle, although completely valid and fairly well tested, requires a thorough understanding and years of experience over many projects.

The information in this book has been researched and verified by myself and my colleagues over a period of more than a decade on the ground in the home of this knowledge: India. Even at this late date in the endeavor, we are certain that our research efforts need to continue to deepen and intensify in the areas of technical and philosophical knowledge and in patient, yet, incessant verification. This book represents my best effort at presenting a most conservative and reliable version of the knowledge at this time. I feel it is a body of knowledge worth presenting.

This book definitely outlines the technology of Vastu architecture, and if this technology is simply expressed and applied with precision, the structure will have value in terms of the ***Vastu effect***. However, the book is not meant to give license to any architect, builder, or potential homeowner to call themselves a Vastu architect.

The Vastu designer bears a great responsibility. To put it simply, if the designer is commissioned to create a Vastu structure, he/she *must* do it completely and correctly. If a professional with no experience in Vastu science has been given the assignment to design and build a Vastu structure, I implore that person to work in concert with a highly experienced Vastu architect until such a time that the expert consultant is convinced that the novice is no longer a novice and can take projects with no consultation.

The main purpose of a Vastu building is to create a living form that will inspire a noble level of consciousness and expression in the beings blessed to live within or even in the proximity of the structure. For this purpose we want to take every step possible to insure the integrity of the final product.

This book does not emphasize the problems or effects of non-Vastu buildings. Vastu science does not usually promote the rectification of buildings but focuses on how to get it right from the beginning. A non-Vastu building is basically unpredictable in terms of the effects on those who occupy it. It is my strong intention to avoid the creation of stress and strain caused by non-scientific opinions applied to non-Vastu buildings. A building that is not compliant with Vastu prescriptions may be challenged in terms of life-supporting energy available to the tenants. On the other hand, such a non-Vastu structure may be a perfectly fine place to occupy. That is all we can say.

May this book be a joy and blessing to all who desire to understand the science of Vastu.

Michael Borden
www.vastu-design.com

Acknowledgments

When I first began my sacred architecture quest, the prospect of finding reliable and comprehensive knowledge of Vastu architecture was dim. Fortunately, during that time I attended a Bharata Natyam dance performance by Sofia Diaz (http://www.sofiayoga.com/). In her introduction to the performance, she spoke of attending a conference on Vastu science in South India presided over by a master architect in the Vastu tradition: Dr. V. Ganapati Sthapati of Mahabalipruam. I offer many thanks to Sofia for helping me find Sthapati, my Vastu guru.

Without Sthapati's tireless and unselfish dedication to Vastu science, this knowledge of infusing the mundane with the divine would most likely have sunk beneath the murky waters of modern life. I am eternally grateful to Sthapati for reviving, preserving, and sharing his knowledge with the world. I encourage the lovers of sacred space worldwide to support his endeavors to preserve and display the tenants of Vastu science at his memorial for Sangakaala Sirpachithan Mamuni Mayan: a structure in Mahabalipruam, Tamil Nadu, India. This structure will house the knowledge of Vastu science for the generations to come. Please see Sthapati's website (www.vastuved.com) or contact me if you would like to donate to this noble endeavor.

My wife, Karen Joost, has been an indispensible partner in this learning process and, I suspect, the source of my good luck throughout the years of this research. She has been a never-ceasing source of encouragement and support in all my adventures and, thankfully, has joined me in many of them, becoming an accomplished Vastu exponent herself. I am very grateful for her companionship and guidance in my work and in my life.

Shyamala Mohanraj, Sofia's Bharata Natyam master teacher, has helped make Chennai our home over the years. She offered us a place to live on the first day we arrived in India and since then has been a constant source of support and love. When we cross the threshold of her home, we always breathe a sigh of relief.

My research was successful with the great help of S. Santhana Krishnan Sthapati, Krithika Karuppiah, Jessie Mercay, and Doris and Harald Buchner, my fellow students of Sthapati, and I am grateful for their efforts in clarifying the knowledge and their readiness to ask and get answers to the many questions we have generated over a decade of research. Santhana and Krithika have established a traditional practice of Vastu temple design worldwide. Jessie has dedicated her life to creating The American University of Mayonic Science and Technology (www.aumscience.com), an excellent resource for all students of Vastu science in the West. Harald and Doris were deeply persistent in asking and getting the answers to the most intriguing questions during our study sessions with Sthapati.

Finally I must send a ray of gratitude to Maharishi Mahesh Yogi, who first raised the lantern of knowledge in my awareness that called me to approach this ancient knowledge of Vastu science.

My Teacher: Dr. V. Ganapati Sthapati

A Short Biography

Born in the year 1927 at Pillayarpatti, a village near Karaikudi, Tamil Nadu, Dr. V. Ganapati Sthapati comes from an illustrious family of temple architects and sculptors. His family lineage stretches back many decades including the Sthapatis who created the great Brihadeeswara Temple of Tanjore, the treasure house of Indian art and architecture. Dr. V. Ganapati Sthapati is the son of Sri Vaidyanatha Sthapati, a renowned sculptor and Sanskrit scholar. Sthapati and his father have made remarkable contributions to the field of art and architecture.

Those who have made the pilgrimage to Sri Ramana Ashram in Tiruvannamalai, Tamil Nadu, will fondly recall the artistic expressions of Sri Vaidyanatha Sthapati in the form of Mother Alagammal's Shrine and the astonishing lifelike sculpture of Sri Ramana at the ashram. Sthapati told me a story of the completion of the statue: Each day, as Sri Vaidyanatha sculpted the image, Sri Ramana would visit the artist at work. One day, as Sri Ramana viewed the work, the saint commented, "Ramana has arrived." At that point Sri Vaidyanatha Sthapati laid down his tools: the image was complete.

The doyen of Indian Vastu Shastra (recently given the title of "Shilpi Guru" by the president of India), Sthapati has been doing research in the field of Vastu science and technology for the past fifty years. A graduate in mathematics and Sanskrit, he is propagating this supreme science in India and abroad. He is chiefly responsible for the resurrection of the works of the Great Brahmarishi Mayan, who was the progenitor of this Indian science and technology and the founder of this rich civilization and culture. At this time Sthapati is erecting a grand tribute to Mayan: a temple in Mahabalipuram, Tamil Nadu, to house the knowledge of Vastu science for all the generations to study.

As the principal of the Government College of Architecture and Sculpture (the only institute of this kind in the world) at Mahabalipuram, Sthapati worked hard for twenty-seven years to restore and elevate the status of the sacred art and architecture by affiliating courses to the University of Madras and offering degree courses. This brought academic status to the age-old tradition of learning and also initiated many young people into this traditional technology.

After retirement from government service, he established Vastu Vedic Trust and Vastu Vedic Research Foundation, their purpose research, development, and globalization of Vastu Shastra. He is also the head of the professional guild named V. Ganapati Sthapati & Associates. This group of talented designers, engineers, and craftsmen work together to create Vastu-inspired temples and other buildings in India and abroad. The palatial buildings of the library and administrative block for Tamil University of Tanjore and the Muthiah Mandram in Madurai speak of his capacity for designing and executing works of stupendous nature. Of particular interest is his monumental Vastu sculpture/building of Thiruvalluvar at the southern tip of India at Kanya Kumari, measuring 133 feet in elevation: a stone Statue of Liberty for India. This colossal marvel has taken him to the pinnacle of his life's achievement as a traditional architect and builder, and commendations and awards have come to him from around the world for this achievement.

He has authored a number of books on the science and technology of Vastu Shastra and has conducted numerous seminars with professionals in a generous effort to make this knowledge available to the world. He has established the International Institute of Mayonic Science and Technology, which conducts workshops and discourses all over the world.

Sthapati held the post of professor and head of the Department of Sthapatya Veda in the World University of Traditional Indian Science, Technology, and Culture in Chennai.

Some of the notable books he has authored include *Iconometry, Temples of Space Science, Building Architecture of Sthapatya Veda,* and *Commentary on Mayan's Aintiram.*

Sthapati has earned a number of titles and awards, including Honorary Fellowship by the Indian Institute of Architects, the National Award for Master Craftsmanship by the president of India, the title of "Shilpi Guru of India," also by the president, and a doctorate degree conferred by the Maharishi Mahesh Yogi Vedic University. He has been awarded the Padma Bhushan award, which is bestowed to recognize distinguished service of a high order to the nation, in any field.

He has worked and done research in the U.S., U.K., Australia, France, Fiji, Germany, Holland, Singapore, Malaysia, Mexico, Guatemala, and Peru. This pulsating and vibrant researcher, sculptor, architect, philosopher, and scientist has produced many startling research discoveries on the intricacies of the traditional art and architecture of India and is quite optimistic that one day Vastu science will be a major influence in the world.

It is with deep gratitude that I introduce you to this great and generous man, Dr. V. Ganapati Sthapati, and his artistic guild of artists/scientists: Manu, blacksmith; Maya, carpenter; Shilpi, architect and sculptor; Twashta, metal work; Vishwagyan, goldsmith.

> *"In the heart cave of the body there is inner space and in that inner-space there is the vibrant thread of consciousness. It is this thread of consciousness that functions as the string of the sarira-vina (bodily instrument)."*

> *"The structure of the Vastu inspired building vibrates with cosmic energy and the bodily instrument resonates with this vibration."*

> *"To create and offer the house of supreme bliss, and to enable us to experience that supreme bliss here in this mundane house itself — these are the prime motives of the Vastu science."*

> — Dr. V. Ganapati Sthapati

For More Information:

- The YogaLife Interview with Dr. Sthapati
- http://www.vastu-design.com/g-interview.htm
- Dr. Sthapati's website: http://www.vastuved.com/
- The www.hinduismtoday.com article on Sthapati:
- http://www.vastu-design.com/ht-article.htm

About the Author

Michael Borden, M.Arch., Ph.D. M.S.T., began his studies in Vastu science in the mid-1990s. In 1999 he traveled to India to study with Dr. V. Ganapati Sthapati of Mahabalipuram, Tami Nadu.

Since then Mr. Borden has made numerous study trips to India and other parts of Asia to deepen his knowledge and experience in the field of Vastu science.

He has designed hundreds of Vastu projects worldwide over the past decade. His website, www.vastu-design.com, is one of the most informative and popular sites available dedicated to Vastu knowledge. Each year he responds to thousands of inquiries from Vastu enthusiasts.

His projects have ranged from simple backyard gazebos and home shrines to custom homes on many continents to multi-building, one hundred thousand square-foot commercial complexes.

Mr. Borden has received a master's in architecture and a Ph.D. in Mayonic science and technology. He is trained in other Eastern arts, including hatha yoga and Thai yoga massage therapy. Please visit the website for more information on Vastu architecture:
www.vastu-design.com

Who Should Read This Book

The principles presented in this text are simple and straightforward. The goal of the book is to de-mystify and clarify an Eastern methodology that has more recently had some misleading and contradictory publications.

Vastu science generates structured creations that are deeply resonant with earthly and cosmic forces. As such, this science is for anyone interested in placing within their environment structures that enhance harmony, prosperity, and love of life.

Also, Vastu science is growing in importance to the Indian diaspora around the world. This knowledge is deeply embedded in the ancient history of the Indian subcontinent. Masters of the discipline preserved and passed on its principles through the cultural mandates of family tradition. Architects, sculptors, masons, carpenters, metal workers, dancers, poets, musicians, all tied their hearts and minds to this knowledge and preserved it for the generations.

However, Britain's two hundred years of occupation of India began to drive a wedge between the Indian people and their mother science of Vastu. During this time traditional lifestyles of all types came under pressure from Western commercial priorities. As a result new generations of Indians began to lose touch with time-tested, established cultural imperatives. Western science and commerce began to set new priorities for Indian life. Within a generation or two, Vastu science fell from view.

Thankfully, the tenants of this science have remained incubating in the minds and hearts of the Indian people, and now many are finding their way back to this knowledge. All gratitude goes to my teacher, Dr. V. Ganapati Sthapati, and his family clan, the Vishwakarmans of South India. Because of them Vastu integrity is safe for the coming generations. Vastu science, a long lost love of the Indian people, is available to those who seek it. I welcome all readers to enjoy this simple and practical science, and I urge all to apply the principles for more joy in life.

Introduction

Many years ago I made my first trip to India after receiving permission from my Vastu mentor, Dr. V. Ganapati Sthapati of Mahabalipuram, to come study. My wife, Karen, and I arrived in Chennai on a hot afternoon and made our way to a dusty hotel near the city center. Little did I know of the heartwarming and intriguing experiences that lay before us in our many visits to that amazing land in the upcoming years.

That afternoon we visited our first ancient temple and felt for the first time the vibration of a Vastu structure. I didn't fully appreciate it at the time, but I have come to know that Vastu energy as unique and enthralling. As I look back on that day, I am deeply thankful to my teacher for sharing the knowledge of how to design such structures, thus making it possible for me to share this profound experience with others.

Once we began our studies with Sthapati (pronounced STAH pa tee), each day we would go to his office, located a couple of blocks from the sparkling Bay of Bengal in Thiruvanmayur, a suburb of Chennai. We would sit with him for a precious few hours in the midst of the hubbub of his bustling office. No matter what was happening that day, Sthapati would stop what he was doing and patiently focus his attention on our studies, speaking at length in his calm, accented voice, illustrating his points with drawings and answering our questions on Vastu science.

True to the form of a master architect/sculptor, Sthapati began with the foundational theories of Vastu science. On many a hot and humid day, we sat with Sthapati as he opened our minds and hearts to his life's mission and passion. It was wonderful knowledge; however, as the days passed and he delved more and more deeply into the theoretical basis of this ancient science, I became restless. I had come to India to learn the technical application of this science so I could return to the West and design and construct buildings vibrant with cosmic energy. I had not anticipated the depth of the knowledge that I was approaching or the length of time it would take to cover it all, and for me the clock was ticking. I felt I had to get the technical information and get back to work! Fortunately, thanks to the gentle counsel of my dear wife, I was able to overcome my impatience and develop an appreciation of first learning the deep theories of this science.

One question I asked Sthapati in those early days was, "What caused the whole process of expression of the universe?" His answer was to quote Khalil Gibran: "Life's longing for Itself!"

Though we call it Vastu science for simplicity's sake, Vastu knowledge encompasses sublime artistic principles as well as scientific principles. In fact, in this discipline no distinction exists between science and art: scientific observation of the natural world is experientially artistic, and vice versa. In the nervous system of an adept Vastu scientist/artist, the manifestations of the universe are experienced and understood fully as a function of his or her unified body-mind-heart. The adept then applies the appropriate principles of manifestation to the creation of new objects that will have the ability to vibrate in deep resonance with the matrices of cosmic energy.

The simple truth of Vastu science is that it has conceived, understood, and applied the most basic formulas governing the ways in which Primal Substance (the pure energy level of the universe) is made manifest as the vast and gross material universe. This science expands on the tenet that no substantial difference exists between subtle and gross forms of life. It is a scientific philosophy of unity of all life forms on all levels for all time.

The ultimate goal of understanding and applying Vastu principles is the full realization of the intrinsic divinity of all life forms.

Thus, Vastu science can be used by any religion but is not limited to any religion. On a gross level, India's Vastu temples, which are the supreme expression of Vastu science, appear to be dedicated to Hindu gods and goddesses. Certainly Vastu science is part of the vast cultural tradition that has risen around the Hindu religion. In fact, we owe our gratitude to the spiritual traditions of the South Indian Shilpi families that have done so much to preserve this knowledge. But Vastu science itself is not religious, nor is it cultural.

Vastu structures are vibrant connections to a universal energy matrix. These structures resonate with the most sublime and powerful forces or laws of nature, which are specified and generated by space/time/light formulas that are the basis of the temple structure. The temple building is an expanded form of the primal life-force law of nature, or "deity," or "seed," within that structure. A seed is a very powerful thing. Within the seed is the whole tree, concentrated and charged with potential. The temple is a fiery center of Spirit density, radiant with Spirit/Essence in harmonic relationship to universal, galactic, solar, earthly, and human life forms.

In Vastu science the technical term Soonyambara translates as "spirit pure" or pure consciousness. Soonyambara is the source of all substance. Sthapati refers to it as "zero space" and defines it as "vacuum," that which is beyond essence. Essence implies existence. Soonyambaram is that pure potential that gives rise to all essence. Within and without the universe, the atom, and every scale in between is swimming in zero space. The universe (Vastu) is expanding into the vacuum of zero space. Also, zero space is found within the micro-universe of the atomic levels.

Sthapati has described the universe as a bubble of rising essence in a sea of Soonyambaram. Out of the vacuum, the universe explodes. The essential substance, the *paramanu* or subtle atom, is the invisible capsule of Cosmic Fire which all forms can call back to as Mother/Father. This seed of Cosmic Fire exists within all forms. It is the essence from Spirit Source of life: the life force within all. Paramanu is the source of all expression, the Divine Micro Being. The cosmos, in total, is the fullest expression of all potential implused at this moment as the Divine marco-Being.

In Vastu science the orthogonal Vastu Purusha Mandala describes the pattern of energy manifesting into substance at the most subtle level. The mandala expresses an order that is self-maintaining. The cubical paramanu form is one with the geometry of the Vastu Purusha Mandala. The cubical "atom" is the basic building block of the universe. This orthogonal pattern is the geometry at the core of all manifestations. It is the geometry of silence. At the center of the paramanu is a thread of light: the Brahma Sutra. This light is the Nataraja: the dancing form of Lord Shiva.

This book is dedicated to the revelation of the divinity within all forms: the foundation of Vastu science and a profound inspiration for all Vastu architects. With the blessing of this science, may we go forward into the ages with peace and harmony for all beings.

We meditate on the glory of the Creator;

Who has created the Universe;

Who is worthy of Worship;

Who is the embodiment of Knowledge and Light.

1. Mayan: Father of Vastu Science

Many people interested in Vastu science arrive at the question, "What is the origin of this knowledge." My teacher, Dr. V. Ganapati Sthapati, was born into the Vishwakarma clan of South India. This clan has been the safe keeper of Vastu knowledge throughout the millenniums. The Vishwakarmans tell us that Vastu science is an ancient knowledge that was envisioned and defined by the great artist and scientist Maharishi Mayan. In the *Mahabharatam*, Veda Vyasa refers to Mayan, the Dhanavaa poet, as Viswakarma, the creator of the cosmos. Hence, Sthapati and his clan of master craftsmen, architects, poets, dancers, sculptors, and musicians, hailing from this ancient tradition founded by Mayan, are called "Vishwakarmans" even today. Sthapati tells us that Mayan lived about 15,000 years ago, establishing Vastu science in the southern part of the Indian subcontinent and in areas further south that have since been covered with the waters of the Indian Ocean.

In the *Ramayana*, Mayan is found to be the father of Mandodari, who was the wife of King Ravenna of Lanka and the architect of the great palace city. Mayan is also referred to in ancient texts by Valmiki and in the Tamil epic *Silappatikaram*.

The *Mayamata* is a work of Mayan. It is a comprehensive treatise on art and architecture, well known and available in the world today, but to the uninitiated, it is very difficult to extract from it a unified body of knowledge that can be technically applied. *Surya Siddhanta*, a treatise on astronomy, is also attributed to Mayan.

Most significantly, Mayan is the author of the *Aintiram*, a treatise on energy, matter, space, time, order, and beauty. In *Aintiram* Mayan explains the subtle universe of atomic and sub-atomic life. He is said to have originated the dancing form of Shiva, Lord Nataraja, which expresses the subtle root form found within the mirco-atomic realms of existence. This is a form that encompasses science, art, and spirit.

In the history of the human race, this Vastu knowledge has thankfully endured owing to the constant efforts of the Vishwakarman clan and continues to offer a clear and simple means by which we can create forms that are in harmony with the laws of nature.

2. Site Selection and Orientation

We live in a modern world with many options available to us for creating comfort in our lives. A Vastu home can also be a great comfort but possibly a comfort of another order. A Vastu structure's main purpose is to facilitate for the occupants an alignment with natural law. We vibrate with energy and life from within. The Vastu structure also vibrates with energy and life. Together the two lives resonate and are uplifted. To achieve this resonance, we set out to create a simple, perfect form in the structure, one that reflects the design goals of Vastu architecture as perfectly as possible. Our first priority is to create a perfect vibrant space that radiates divine energy at its core and then to humbly live around the periphery of that sublime space. This space will nourish our soul, and when our soul is nourished, all other aspects of life flourish.

The first step in creating a Vastu structure is to locate a suitable place on Earth for it. Vastu science considers Earth a living organism, which is embedded in space and a part of the cosmic, living body of the universe. When we initiate a project to place a Vastu structure on Earth, it is important that we honor Mother Earth by giving attention to how and where we place the structure.

The chief elements of site selection are the following:

1) Orientation of the structure and the shape and orientation of the site
2) General slope of the land and adjacent topography
3) Outstanding natural elements on the land or nearby
4) Relationship of the structure to the eastern horizon
5) Relationship with existing or potential roads
6) Condition of the soil
7) Existence of man-made elements
8) Landscape trees and shrubs

Orientation of the structure and the shape and orientation of the site

With respect to our location in the universe, there is no north, south, east or west, just the origin-center of the universe body and the ever expanding outer edges. The underlying geometry of a

Vastu structure reflects this kind of center-oriented paradigm. However, Vastu science gives recognition to "directional" existence within the context of an "embodied" form—the Earth or a building or a human being—in relationship to the Energetic Grid that expresses on the surface of the planet and in the solar core of our planetary system.

Vastu science delineates eight yonis, which are directions or life-energy lines of orientation: east, dwajam (flagstaff); southeast, dhuumam (smoke); south, simham (lion); southwest, swaanam (dog); west, vrushabham (bull), northwest, kharam (ass); north, gajam (elephant); and northeast, kaakam (crow). Within the built space, the eight directions are always expressed and honored by floor plan layouts.

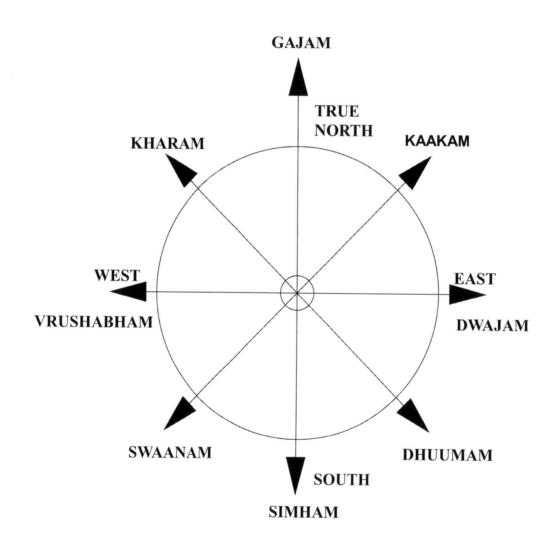

Illustration 1

Vastu buildings must be oriented such that they have an almost parallel relationship to the cardinal points of the compass: north, south, east, and west. Perfect alignment with the cardinal points of the compass is called Suddha Praachee. This perfect alignment is suitable for temples. Also, in Mansara and some Vastu Shastras, true east is suitable for occupants who seek liberation from earthly bonds. Esa Prachee is the preferred orientation for a secular structure. This orientation rule will be discussed further in this text.

The first rule of orientation: That the structure sits on the Earth with a direct relationship to *true north* is of primary importance. True north is also known as map north or geographic north. If you look on a globe, it is the point on the Earth where all the longitude lines meet in the north.

Another north, magnetic north, is the direction that the north arrow points in a compass. *Magnetic north must not be used for orientation of a Vastu structure.* If you use magnetic north, you may not have the correct orientation for the structure.

The Earth is a magnetic body. If you see the shape of the magnetic field of a common bar magnet, you will see that the field radiates in a circular pattern from each pole. The north arrow of the compass points along the magnetic field lines of the magnetic north pole. For example, in the Western United States the difference between true north and magnetic north (called the declination) can be as much as thirteen degrees east. This means magnetic north is pointing thirteen degrees east of true north!

All geographic maps are laid out with respect to true north. (If you have an informal site map for a plot of land, always confirm that the north arrow is correctly representing true north and not just an approximation by the person who made the map.) In the northern hemisphere, the lodestar, Polaris (the North Star), gives us the direction of true north. The lodestar is a star that is used as a reference point in navigation or astronomy. If you locate Polaris in the night sky and face it, you are looking directly to true north. However, it is difficult to set a building orientation by Polaris unless you are a professional surveyor.

Note: The Vastu orientation rules universally applied for both Northern and Southern Hemispheres. Once you know the direction of true north, you can determine if it will be possible to orient the structure and its protecting Vastu fence with a close parallel relationship to true north for any particular plot of land. If you find that this will not be possible, then the plot of land must be dropped from consideration for the Vastu structure.

Defining "facing" of a building:

Once the exact orientation of the site is clear, the "facing" direction of the building can be chosen. The facing of the building is determined by the location of the front of the structure and the main entry door.

The benefits that the structure can bring to the occupants are dependent on the orientation of the face of the building. Each facing—east, north, west, and south—has a different and positive, influence. The general influences are as follows: east facing, physical comfort and mental peace; north facing, wealth; west facing, material growth and prosperity; south facing, salvation, freedom from earthly worries. In most cases it is best to choose an east, north, or west facing orientation if the occupants are householders living normal lives in the world. A south facing house is better for individuals not interested in worldly affairs but in a more monastic way of life.

In a Vastu structure, the face of the building is well defined by the Vastu architect, with no ambiguity in the design. The mandala of the house is chosen for a particular facing and all elements of the structure respond to that orientation.

For an existing building, the face of the building can be ambiguous. The facing must be determined by observation of the following elements:

A) The house has an architectural "front." When you approach the house it usually will project an image that tells one "this is my face."

B) The location of the main, formal entry door will reinforce the notion of the facing of the building. This is the door that says, "I am the public entrance." Locating this door will give you the front of the house.

As a refinement to these points, the actual physical front of the main door is not a ruling factor for defining the facing of the structure. If the face of a house is determined to be in one direction, but the main door faces another, then the facing is still determined by the architectural front of the house, not the door. If the front of the house is to the south, but an entry extension allows the front *door* on the south side of the house to face east, this is still considered a south-facing house and a south entrance. This is because the main entry door is located on the south side of the structure.

Sometimes the main front door is not used much. For example, homeowners like to enter the house directly from the parking area. Usually this parking area is not at the front door of the house. If this is the case, the location of the oft-used entry needs to be taken into consideration in terms of the influence of the entry position of the door, but the facing of the house would remain that which is determined by the criteria mentioned above.

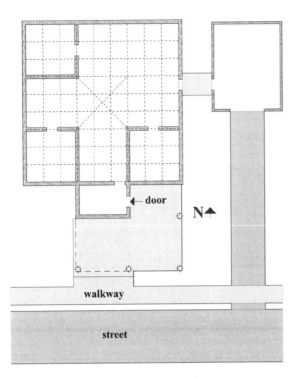

Illustration 2
South Facing Building
East facing door on South side
of house is actually a <u>south</u> entrance

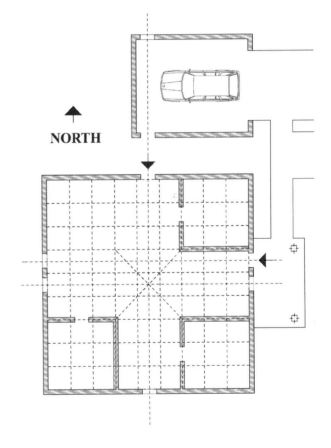

Illustration 3
Two doors in auspicous locations
for conditions where both doors
will be used often

Fine-tuning the orientation

Esa Prachee: In a secular structure, the orientation is influenced by a prescribed rotation (or deflection) of the building from perfect alignment with the cardinal points. In an east- or west-facing building, the prescribed rotation is one and a half degrees *counterclockwise.* This deflection of east towards northeast is Esa Praachee. In a north- or south-facing building, the prescribed rotation is one and a half degrees *clockwise.* Rotations up to ten degrees are acceptable, but not recommended.

A simple way to understand the effect of incorrect orientation is to use the example of adjusting a radio tuning dial. As we turn the knob on the radio away from the correct frequency position for a particular radio signal, the quality of the reception deteriorates and distorts. The same is true for alignment of buildings on the Earth. The more rotated a building is from the cardinal directions, the more distortion within the energy field of the structure.

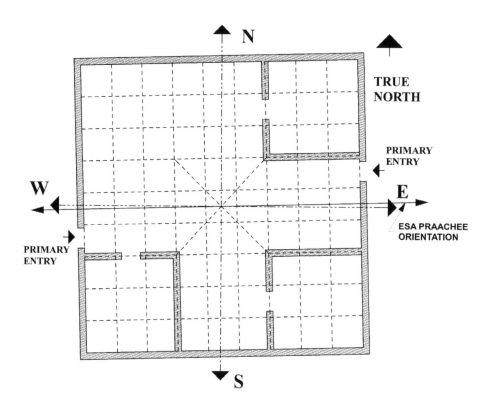

Illustration 4a
East or west facing building
rotated 1.5 degrees
counter-clockwise

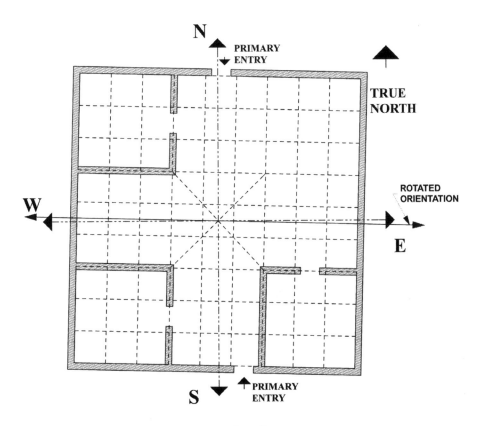

Illustration 4b
North or South facing building
rotated 1.5 degrees
clockwise

Orientations rotated more than ten degrees toward the southeast, southwest, northwest and north-east are not recommended. *[See illustration on next page.]*

Correct orientation is necessary because in the technology of the science, a living Vastu structure is constructed with respect to a Vastu Purusha Mandala (VPM). The VPM is a geometric pattern that is expressed in the three dimensions. The Earth is a living Vastu structure and, as such, is rooted in a VPM matrix: the underlying geometry that gives rise to its form. This Earth VPM, the seed of which originates from the energetic fiery core of the planet, is expressed in orthogonal energy lines across the surface of the Earth. The lines are similar in concept to what we know as longitude and latitude lines. Vastu science refers to the longitudinal and latitudinal lines as Dirkha Rekha and Aksha Rekha respectively. Energy deep within the Earth is expressed on the surface of the planet, fuming out along these lines. The Earth grid is also a receptor of solar, lunar, and stellar radiation to nourish and energize the planet.

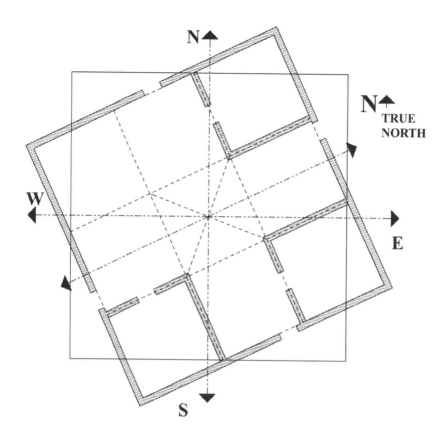

Illustration 5
Example of an over-rotated building

When we place a Vastu structure on the Earth, it is necessary that the VPM of the structure and the VPM of the Earth come into resonance. This is done by aligning the two geometries in a near parallel fashion. This alignment brings the structure into resonance with the planet and Earth energy can flood into the structure. This is the reason Vastu architects will not allow a building to be rotated significantly out of alignment from the cardinal points of the compass.

The shape of the plot, determined by the legal boundaries of land, is an important consideration. In general, rectangular- or square-shaped plots are most easily accepted for a Vastu structure. A large plot of land provides more flexibility to make corrections for Vastu considerations. In practical application a large plot of land allows rotation of the structure for correct orientation. Also, the larger plot will allow for the creation of a perfectly correct Vastu wall around the structure. The plot of land could even be irregularly shaped, and still it could be possible to correct all issues by creating a perfect universe for the house by surrounding it with a proper Vastu wall within the legal boundaries of the plot. However, even if we have established a perfect Vastu compound for the structure on an irregularly shaped plot of land, a wall on the legal boundary should be avoided, because such a wall will set up dissonant vibrations on the plot.

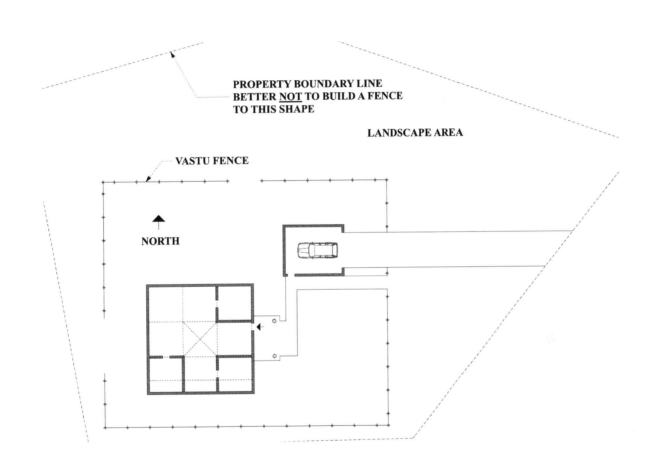

**Illustration 6 - Large, irregular plot of
land with a Vastu house and yard placed
comfortably within the boundary lines**

Careful consideration should be given to whether the structure and a properly located Vastu fence can be constructed on the site. A small plot of land can be more challenging because it may be more difficult to create a proper Vastu compound within the legal boundaries of the site. Also, on small plots of land, greater pressure exists to create a boundary wall for privacy on the legal sides of the plot. Such a boundary wall will most likely not have resonance with the Vastu structure and may also create an enclosed compound the shape of which will be inauspicious. In small plots of land, square and rectangular shapes are recommended, with good orientation in relation to the cardinal points of the compass. All irregular shapes should be avoided unless, somehow, you can create a perfectly oriented structure with a proper Vastu wall around it.

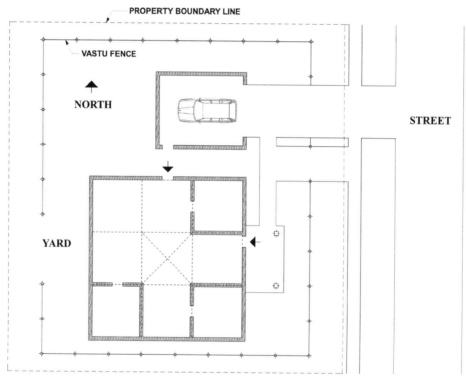

Illustration 7 - Subdivision lot with no challenges for Vastu structure and fence

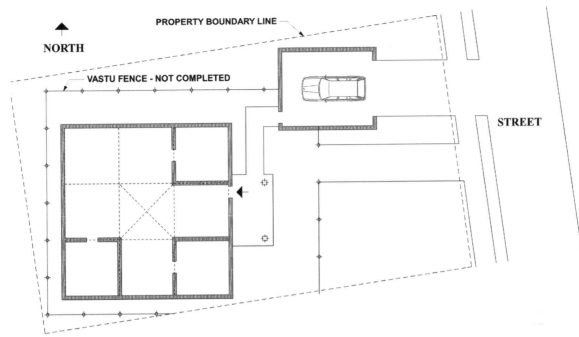

**Illustration 8 - Subdivision lot with a forced
relationship to the Vastu house and fence**

As a footnote:

In general, correct orientation begins with correct layout of a town settlement. If a settlement layout and orientation is non-compliant with Vastu principles, there will be problems throughout its history.

General slope of the land itself and adjacent topography

In general, flat or gently sloping land is preferred for a Vastu structure. Land sloping down to east, northeast, north and northwest is acceptable for a Vastu site. These are the simple rules in terms of acceptable topography for a Vastu project.

It is recommended that the slope of the land is not excessive. Ideally the slope should not exceed five to ten degrees. Flat land is also good for a Vastu structure; however, one should observe the slope of land directly adjacent to the building site. If an existing condition violates the Vastu prescriptions, the land may not be acceptable. For example, if the general pattern of sloping land surrounding an acceptable plot is in a downward direction that is not recommended—southeast, south, southwest and west—then the overall influence on the accepted plot of land may be less than desirable.

A hilltop, where all directions are sloping downward from the structure, is not ideal. However, if the area at the top of the hill is large and a generous Vastu compound can be created for the structure, the location could be acceptable after careful consideration by the Vastu professional.

It is acceptable to make *small* changes in slope conditions on a site to rectify an existing condition that is barely non-compliant. Adding or subtracting large quantities of earth is not recommended. Vastu science regards the Earth as a living being and holds the existing natural conditions of the site to be an expression of the intrinsic Earth energy expressed at that location. Gross changes to the topography of the site, does nothing to change the underlying Earth energies that caused the natural formations on the site.

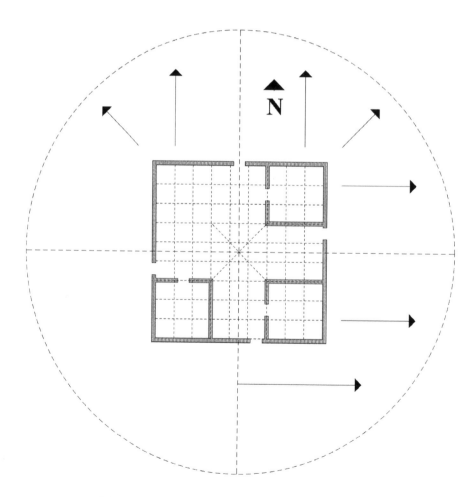

**Illustration 9 - Arrows indicate downward
slopes that are considered auspicious**

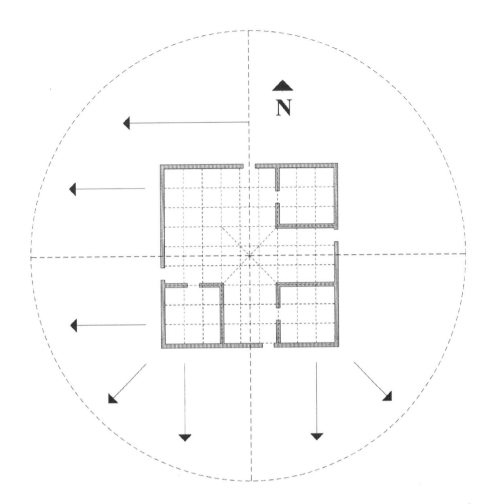

**Illustration 10 - Arrows indicate downward
slopes that are NOT considered auspicious**

Outstanding natural elements on or nearby the land

Nature elements, lakes, rivers, boulders, trees should be carefully observed.

In general, water bodies less than one thousand feet from the site are allowed only in the northeast area of the Vastu site. When we are placing the Vastu structure on the site, the centerline of the structure in both directions should not extend into a body of water. Also, the centerline of the front door, extended in both directions through the structure to the landscape behind the structure and outward from the door into the landscape, should not extend into a body of water for one thousand feet.

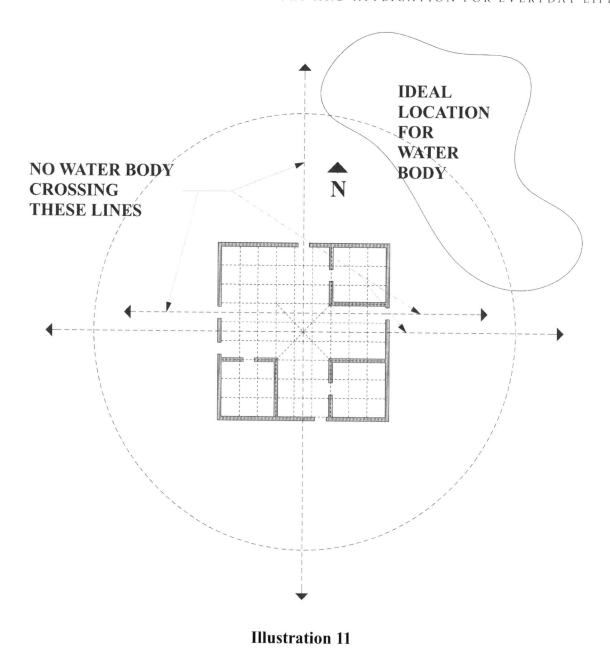

Illustration 11

A site with water courses, rivers, creeks, and irrigation ditches can run on the north side of the Vastu structure, and the flow is best if running toward east and/or clockwise around the site. A site with water courses running from the northwest flowing south, southwest flowing east, and southeast flowing north are not recommended. Depending on the size, direction of flow, and location of a water course, it may be possible to allow it in any direction. A consultation with a Vastu expert is necessary.

A site with a close mountain range to the west or south is acceptable. However, a site with a mountain range in close proximity to the east and north is usually not recommended unless it is analyzed and approved by a Vastu consultant.

The main axes of the structure are the east/west axis, the north/south axis, and the axis running through the house from the centerline of the front door. These axes must remain unobstructed by large rocks, tree trunks, or any other large object. *[See illustration on next page.]*

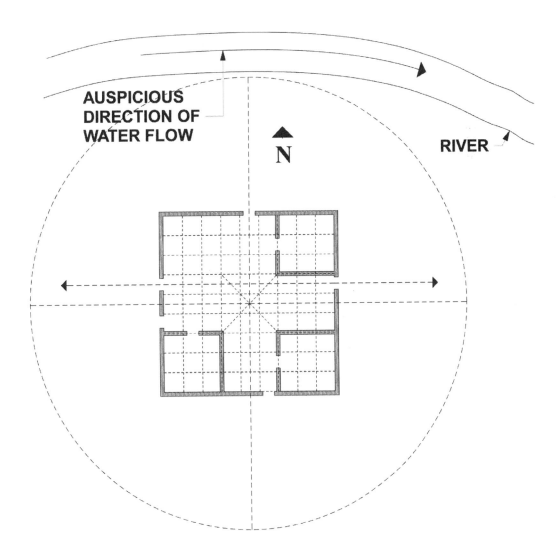

**Illustration 12 - Accepted location and
directional flow of nearby river**

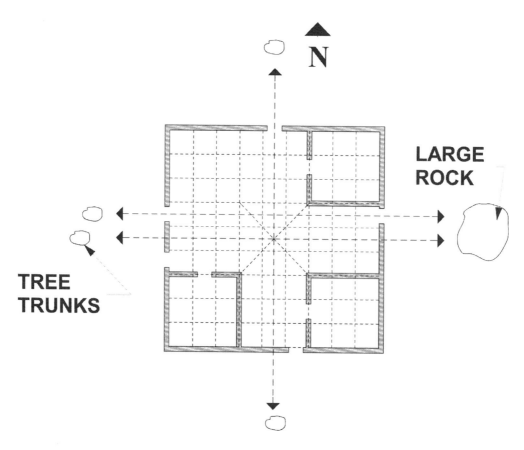

**Illustration 13 - Axis lines of structure
shall NOT be obstructed by landscape objects**

Relationship of the structure to the eastern horizon

The general rule is to place the house in an area where the eastern sun is not blocked significantly. The rising sun is a valuable asset in terms of Vastu architecture. The ideal is for the structure to be exposed to the sun as it rises over the horizon in the morning. However, it is acceptable to have the sun's rays within an hour or two of sunrise.

Throughout the year the sunrise location shifts in the east from southeast to northeast. At times a building or natural object may delay exposure to the sunrise for a few days or a week. This condition is not a problem.

Relationship with existing or potential roads

A roadway should not come directly toward a site. The reason is that a road is an energy conduit. The energy of vehicles in motion and the energy of the attention of humans in the vehicles directed forward will disrupt the peaceful atmosphere of the Vastu structure. Sometimes, depending on the configuration and size of the site, the road may be allowed to run to a portion of the site as long as it is not directed at the main Vastu structure and compound. *[See also illustration on next page.]*

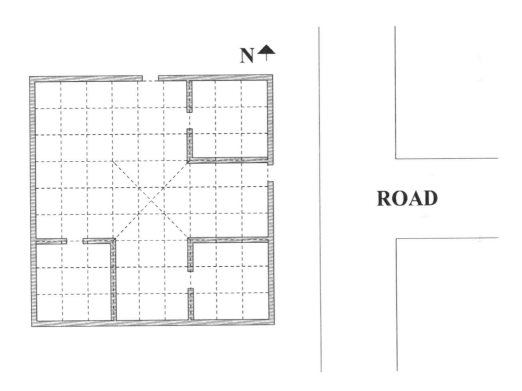

Illustration 14a - T-junction
NOT recommended

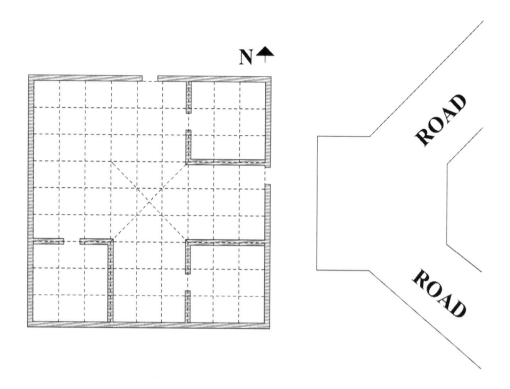

Illustration 14b - Y-junction
NOT recommended

Condition of the soil

The basic requirement for good soil condition on a Vastu site is 1) it should have good bearing capacity, 2) the plant and animal life on and around it should reflect good fertility—for example, the plants should be lush and fragrant, 3) the land should have a good odor, 4) the area should be spacious and level, and 5) sub-soil water should flow clockwise.

Note: Always have the site soil tested for soil-bearing capacity by licensed engineers.

Here are a few basic soil tests that can be done for Vastu evaluation:

Test #1: Dig a pit with length, width, and depth two feet nine inches each; then refill the pit with the excavated soil. If the re-filled pit has a mound of soil rising out of the ground, this is considered a good condition. If the pit is filled to level, it is satisfactory. If the soil level is below the top of the pit when refilled, the soil is substandard.

It could be that this test was used to determine the soil-bearing capacity in olden days. In terms of this test, *the final decision of soil integrity should be left to the professional consultation of the civil and structural engineers.*

Test #2: In terms of soil fertility, the best test is to review the plant life on the site and see if it is full and healthy and fruit bearing. Another traditional test for the fertility influences on the site is to allow a herd of cows, including a bull, on the site. If the activities of the cows and bull express affection and procreation, then the site is considered good for habitation. It is said that the good spiritual vibration on the site is responsible for such amorous activity of the herd.

Test #3: Dig a pit with the same dimensions as in Test #1. Fill the pit with water and throw some flower petals on the surface of the water. Patiently and quietly observe the direction of rotation of the water in the pit. A clockwise rotation is a positive indication of good energy, the site suitable for a Vastu structure. If the rotation is counterclockwise or nil, it is considered a negative result.

Test #4: The toxic nature of the soil is checked with the "wick test." This test is accomplished by floating four flames on the water of the second pit. You can use tea candles on a plate or some other method of achieving this condition. If all four flames remain lit for a period of ten minutes or so, then the test indicates no toxic influences. If two flames remain active, the test is acceptable but not excellent. If all flames extinguish, it indicates the presence of some negative fumes issuing from the soil.

Important: Observe the wind conditions in the area of the pit during these tests. The pit must be sheltered from the influence of the wind. Don't fill the pit completely full; keep the water six to nine inches down from the top, and shelter the pit from breezes long enough to observe the rotation of the flower petals. If you get a negative result and you have a large enough site, you can try a pit in another location.

The Vastu texts do not recommend building on sites where the following conditions exist:

1) Marshy, wet soils

2) Soils heavily composed of clay (note: in Iowa, U.S., I have built a number of Vastu structures in soil conditions that did have quite a bit of clay. I did not see a negative effect. It could be that clay soils present structural challenges that were considered unsuitable for ancient structures.)

3) Soils with trash, bones, toxic substances, and charcoal

4) Sites infested with rats, biting ants, snakes, or frogs

5) Land that is sparse and/or filled with thorn-bearing brush or trees

Man-made elements

All enclosed space is living space. Every structure emanates an influential vibration. Buildings such as factories, mortuaries, trash processing plants, etc. should not be adjacent to a Vastu site. A simple evaluation of the function of the building will review the nature of influence emanating from it.

A Vastu site should not have extensive shadowing or face a large building, especially a church or temple.

The basic goal of site evaluation is to find a plot of land that has pleasant vibrations suitable for a Vastu structure. Artificial soil amendment and topographic modifications are not recommended. The basic rule is that if the site does not meet the proper requirements, reject it and go on to another.

Landscape trees and shrubs

Trees and shrubs, vegetables and fruits, all have energetic influences within a Vastu landscape. The traditional Vastu texts include information on this subject, but to date I have not been able to finalize a detailed and validated list of recommended vegetation in the vicinity of a Vastu structure. Some general comments, however, can be made and some specific vegetation that can be defined:

1) Sweet-smelling flowers and fruits have a positive influence.

2) Thorny or poisonous trees, shrubs, and flowers are not recommended.

3) Fruit-bearing trees are good on the east.

4) Some consistently recommended plants are grapes, neem, lime (however, this plant can have thorns), tulsi, mango, bilva, jasmine (mullai), pomegranate, kondrai.

5) Some plants consistently *not* recommended are palmyra, agaththi, oleander, erucku, tamarind, banyan, peepal.

However, this is not to say the plants not recommended are "bad" in general. Every plant has its place in nature and should be honored. In fact, some of the above mentioned plants in the "do not use" list are considered sacred and welcome within a temple complex.

Practical considerations

Sometimes the choice of available land is limited. It might be that we decide to choose a site that doesn't fulfill all the above requirements. It is very important to consult with an expert Vastu practitioner before making a commitment to purchase a site. Under such circumstances the Vastu consultant can weigh all the elements of the site and make a final recommendation based on knowledge and experience. Building a structure is a big commitment financially; a little patience at the beginning of the project is an excellent beginning.

■ What you learned in this chapter:

1) Orientation is a function of the facing direction of the building.

2) Correct building orientation is directly related to the cardinal points of the compass: north, south, east, and west.

3) Each building orientation direction has specific influences for the occupants.

4) The topography of the Vastu site should be level or higher in the south and/or west and lower in the north and/or east.

5) Landscape elements such as bodies of water, roads, mountains, large trees, and rocks need to be located correctly with respect to the Vastu structure.

6) The Vastu structure should have reasonably good exposure to the sunrise.

7) Soil conditions on the Vastu site should be investigated for negative elements, such as marshy conditions, pollution, etc.

8) Trees and shrubs on the property can have an effect on the residents of a Vastu structure.

3. Building Design Basics

In applying Vastu principles to a structure we shall consider the following:

1) The Vastu Purusha Mandala

2) Vastu units of measure

3) Doors and entrance locations

4) Resonance with VPM: wall location

5) Prescribed plan patterns and proportions

6) Wall thickness

7) The enclosing Vastu fence

8) Practical construction considerations

9) Room layout according to function

10) Location of polluting elements in the floor plan

11) Stairs

12) Zones of flexibility

13) Bed location

14) Mechanical room

15) Location of service structures

16) Location of wells

The Vastu Purusha Mandala

When we erect the four walls and roof of a building, we enclose Universal Space. At this point the structure becomes a living organism. In Vastu architecture the living organism created is a vibrant structure embodied with a light-energy core at its center, the Brahmastan. Just as the light atom within our human heart structure gives us the ability to resonate with Source Energy, the man-made Vastu building also has a structural geometric resonance with Source Energy, which gives it life. This resonance endows the building with an atmosphere of vibrant peace. Living in such a structure has a purpose beyond shelter and comfort. Our habitation offers a constant opportunity to humbly visit at the altar of Universal Life: the energy generated within the Brahmastan. This central space is a powerful energy core: the heart of the structure. From this center, earth and cosmic energies radiate through the whole building and out into the surrounding site. Having established the silent center, the Brahmastan, the occupants may live their simple lives around its radiance and automatically come into relationship with it. This is the ideal of Vastu living.

Every Vastu structure has a subtle geometry that governs its form. This geometry is called a Vastu Purusha Mandala (VPM). The VPM is a simple orthogonal (square or rectangular) form that defines the pathway that formless pure energy takes to manifest into spatial form. All gross physical forms have an origin in the subtle seed geometry of the VPM.

The principles expressed in the VPM are at the foundation of Vastu science. However, the origin of the knowledge of the VPM is difficult to pinpoint because it is ancient. Over thousands of years, the preservation of the knowledge has depended on deeply mythological language. In the *Brihat Samhita,* a sixth century treatise by Varahamihira, we find the classic Asian "story" of the origin of knowledge of the VPM. It tells of a powerful force of nature producing an overwhelming disturbance in the celestial space. In response to this spreading force, it is said that celestial luminaries called devas (intrinsic laws of nature having manifested in the primal expression from Source) joined in unison to control and stabilize it. By subduing and stabilizing this powerful energy through exertion of a native order involving attention, force, and love, the devas patterned a manifestation code or diagram. This code is the VPM: the seed pattern of pure cosmic energy being formed into solid matter and also a diagram of the subtle order of the manifest universe. In this diagram, we find the devas (laws of nature), such as Surya, Indra, Gandharva, and Vayu, (forty-five in all), each with a designated location within the outer ring of the Paramasayika Vastu Mandala .

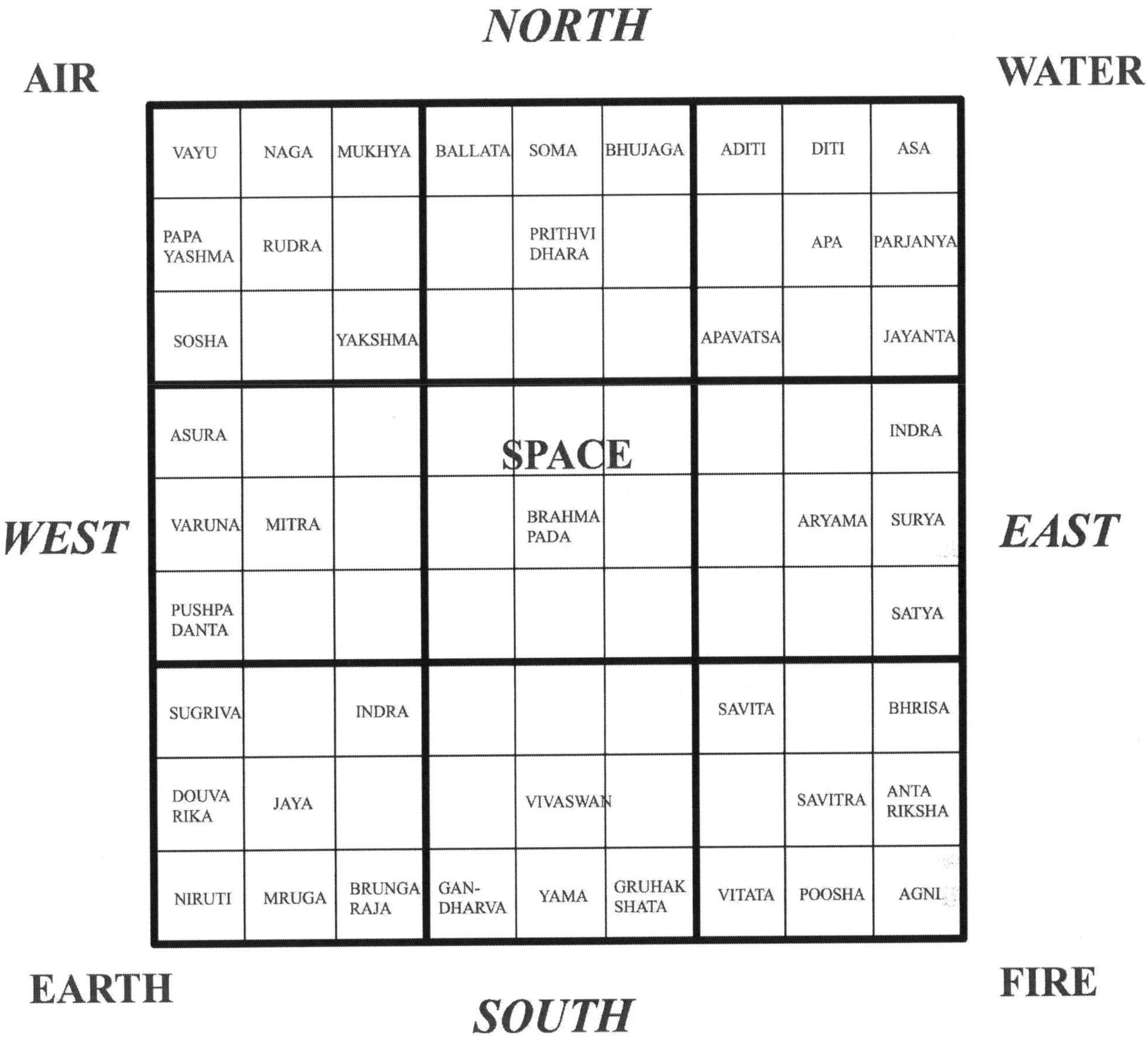

NORTH

AIR   **WATER**

VAYU	NAGA	MUKHYA	BALLATA	SOMA	BHUJAGA	ADITI	DITI	ASA
PAPA YASHMA	RUDRA			PRITHVI DHARA			APA	PARJANYA
SOSHA		YAKSHMA				APAVATSA		JAYANTA
ASURA				**SPACE**				INDRA
VARUNA	MITRA			BRAHMA PADA			ARYAMA	SURYA
PUSHPA DANTA								SATYA
SUGRIVA		INDRA				SAVITA		BHRISA
DOUVA RIKA	JAYA			VIVASWAN			SAVITRA	ANTA RIKSHA
NIRUTI	MRUGA	BRUNGA RAJA	GAN-DHARVA	YAMA	GRUHAK SHATA	VITATA	POOSHA	AGNI

WEST   **EAST**

EARTH   **FIRE**

SOUTH

Illustration 15
VASTU PURUSHA MANDALA

When energy expresses as matter, it takes on more qualities. These qualities can be good or bad, life supporting or life damaging, intrinsically organized or entropic. Cosmic and Earth forces can be positive or negative, depending on the point of view of the nervous system subject to them. For example, a light breeze in summer is a welcome relief from a hot day for a human, but if we take the same force of nature and increase the energy multifold, it can become a destructive hurricane that destroys human systems. On the other hand, the light breeze may have no clear macro-environmental effect, but a hurricane may purify and rebalance a polluted and strained ecosystem.

By applying the principles of the VPM, Vastu science positively controls the type and intensity of energy captured within the built environment.

The spatial universe is awash in cosmic atoms that are the seeds of manifest life. This atom is in the form of the cubical VPM. This space atom is also at the core of the living heart of every being. It is the geometric tuning fork that calls forth life by vibrating with life unmanifest. Vastu science enlists the technology of the space atom mandala to create new forms that resonate with that unmanifest energy.

There are two primary types of VPM. One is a square pattern of eight by eight modules called Mandukapada Mandala, and one is nine-by-nine modules called Paramasayika Mandala. (There are also non-primary mandalas ranging from one by one to thirty-two by thirty-two.)

Mandukapada Mandala is subtle and Paramasayika Mandala is gross. Mandukapada Mandala is a pattern expressing the early progression of energy into matter, that of the subtle universe. Paramasayika Mandala is later in the progression: the gross expression of matter. Mandukapada is used to pattern sacred buildings. The energy in these buildings is highly spiritual and not ideal for human habitation. We can visit these spaces for inspiration but not reside in them. Paramasayika is used to pattern secular buildings that have energy levels most conducive to human peace and prosperity.

The VPM is divided into concentric zones specific to a quality of energy predominant in that area. The Brahma Pada is the zone of divine energy. This zone is the heart of the structure. The Deivika Pada is the zone of celestial energy adjacent to the Brahma Pada. The Manusha Pada is the zone of human energy. The Paisachika Pada is the zone of mineral energy. The outer two zones, Manusha and Paisachika, are ideally the areas in which the mundane activities of daily life take place within the structure. Illustrated below are the two basic Vastu mandalas with a diagram of their respective energy zones.

MANDUKA VASTU MANDALA
8 X 8 modulated spaces

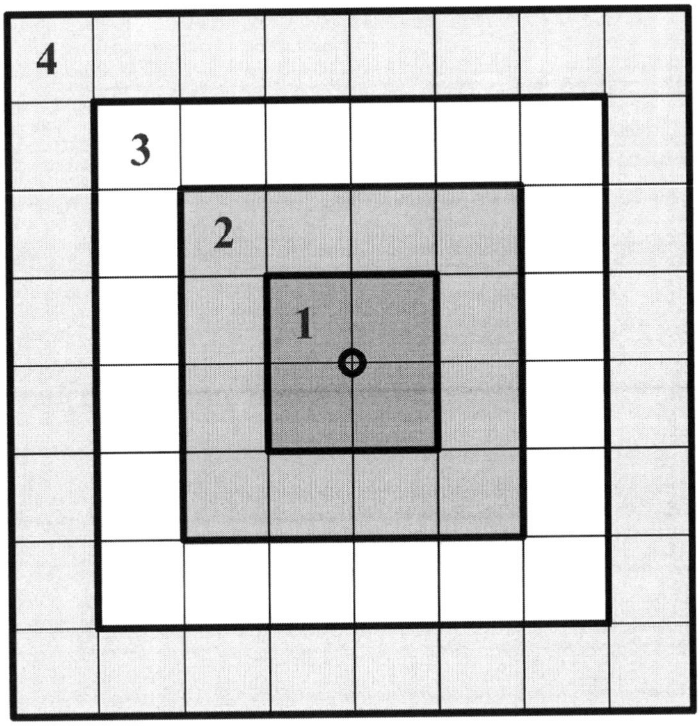

Illustration 16a

1 - Brahma Pada: 4 padas - God
2 - Deivika Pada: 12 padas - Celestial
3 - Manusha Pada: 20 padas - Human
4 - Paisachika Pada: 28 padas - Mineral
TOTAL = 64 padas

PARAMA SAAYIKA VASTU MANDALA
9 x 9 modulated spaces

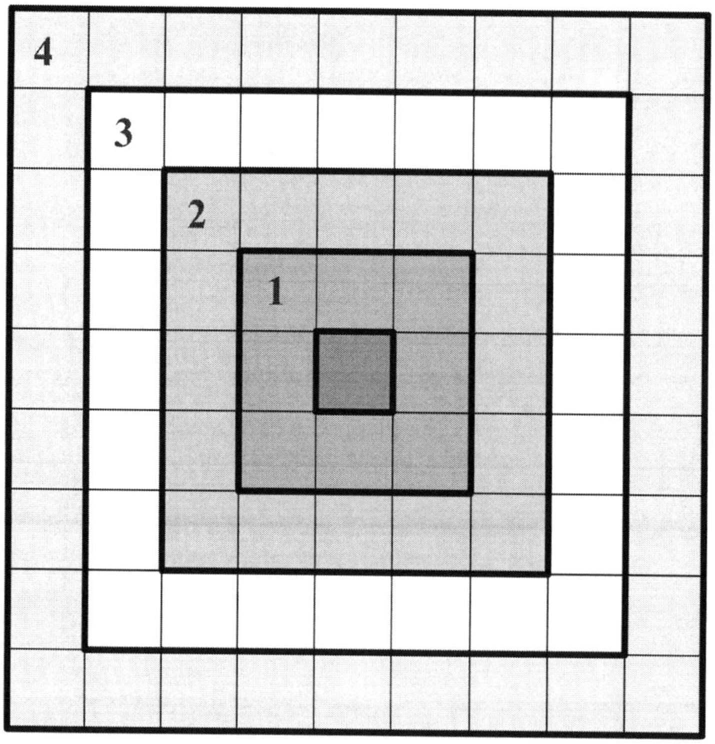

Illustration 16b

1 - Brahma Pada: 9 padas - God
2 - Deivika Pada: 16 padas - Celestial
3 - Manusha Pada: 24 padas - Human
4 - Paisachika Pada: 32 padas - Mineral
TOTAL = 81 padas

In his excellent treatise, *The Building Architecture of Sthapatya Veda*, Dr. V. Ganapati Sthapati speaks of the Vastu Purusha Mandala:

These padas are interpreted as consisting of concentric square belts (conduits for the flow of energy) going around the central core space with a concentrated energy center called Brahma Bindu or Brahma Padam,(this point is OM, a composite element of light and sound). The adjacent belt is called Deivika Padam (the field of luminosity). The third belt is Manusha Padam (the field of consciousness), and the fourth and final one is Paisachika Padam (the field of gross matter). They are primary wave patterns emanating from the inner space of individual beings and from the outer space of universal being, the cosmos. This order is "dharma." The technical name for it is "Vastu dharma."

...at the atomic level, the concentric square belts are wiry—a bundle of energy wires woven into threads running parallel to each other and also diagonally from corner to corner. In Tamil this particular "knot" is called Brahma Granthi—energy knot. They are called Rekhas in the shastras. The diagonal rekhas are also called Rajjus, denoting lines or conduits or nerves for flow of energy. In short, the Vastu Purusha Mandala is a bundle of energy lines (conduits) packed inside the cube, the flow of which gives rise to orderly form in the world of reality.

Vastu units of measure

Each VPM for a particular structure is carefully calibrated for specific beneficial effects. The frequency of the mandala is set by the *dimension of the perimeter* expressed in traditional units of Vastu science.

Dr. V. Ganapati Sthapati from *The Building Architecture of Sthapatya Veda*:

The system is unique, in that it is time that is the basic unit of measure...This concept has paved the way for the emergence of a rare system of units of time and space, where time and space are equated; the time units are converted into space units and applied to create tri-dimensional material objects...

Time (rhythm) units are..."taala." This (measure) is prevalent in the fields of music, dance, and poetry. The same taala unit is applied in the design of buildings as well as town and city layouts. Vastu mathematics—numerical at a subtle level, but geometrical at application level—has its source in the concept of time as a unit of measure. The science of mathematics is rooted...in the concept of time as the vibration of energy and matter. Energy changes into time causing space, which takes spatial (material) forms.

The generation of forms out of the vibration of energy-space is identified and quantified by Mayan as "eight" and "multiples of eight," in that order. Hence, in the table of time units and space units, you find the evolution of the measure starting from zero and evolving into forms in terms of multiples of eight...the nature of the number eight is to turn into form.

This is the basic formula of rhythms influencing the growth of all animate forms in a mathematical order, and this is the fundamental measure adopted by the dancers, musicians, poets, sculptors, and architects for the development of all artistic forms that they experience and generate from within.

The Vastu Shastras and Mayamatam say all objects are known by their dimensions. In other words the dimensions are an expression of a particular energy quality of an object. The dimensions, when blended with geometry in a three-dimensional object, give integrity and genuineness.

Dimensions are created by Vastu "space units." These units of measure are based on dimensions derived from basic natural forms:
(From Dr. V. Ganpati Sthapati's *Sirpachennool*, published by the Directorate of Technical Education, Chennai)

Table of space units

8 anus = 1 "car dust"

8 car dusts = 1 immu

8 immu = 1 ellu (seseme seed)

8 ellu = 1 nel (unhusked paddy grain)

8 nel = 1 viral (finger measure)

6 viral = 1 taalam

12 viral = 1 vitasti

24 viral = 1 kishku hastam

Viral (or angula), taalam, vitasti, and kishku hastam are the basic units of measure we use for Vastu structures:

viral = 1⅜"

taalam = 8¼"

vitasti = 1'4½"

hastam = 2'9"

Some other Vastu units used are the following:

8 kishku hastam = 1 dandam = 22'0"

8 dandam = 1 rajju = 176'0"

3. BUILDING DESIGN BASICS

In general we use large units for large objects and small units for small objects. For example, you would not use angulas (1⅜") to set the measure of a town wall or large house. (This practice of using hastam, vitasti, and taalam units of measure is a protocol I personally developed after many years of experience attempting to apply Vastu dimensions to conventionally built structures.)

Kishku hastam is universally accepted for use for all Vastu structures. Other hastam can be used for specific structures, for example forts, palaces, water tanks, and streets, but these will not be considered here. We can apply kishku hastam to all of these structures.

The Vastu Purusha Mandala of the structure is assigned a perimeter value that is measured in whichever Vastu unit of measure is chosen by the architect. For example, 55 kishku hastams (55 x 2'9") would give a perimeter value of 151'3" or 37'9¾" on each side of a square mandala.

In building techniques it is always a challenge to achieve one hundred percent accuracy to a pre-scribed dimension. In general, building material properties cause inconsistent measurement values. Wood can shrink or expand depending on the site conditions. Bricks can be inconsistent in size. The constructor, in laying out the building foundation or walls, may not be able to always set the dimensions for construction of material in perfection.

The Vastu builder must follow certain protocols (to be detailed later) in order to achieve a high degree of accuracy. The strong intention must be to keep the dimensions in integrity throughout the construction process and the final result should be acceptable.

For buildings it is best to use kishku hastams as a first choice instead of ½ (vitasti) or ¼ (taalam) hastam or 1 angula because, when finally laying out the structure of the building, the larger unit would make it easier to achieve a high degree of accuracy in keeping to the prescribed Vastu units.

For example,

55 hastas (hasta = 2'-9") = 151'3" perimeter value

If during construction the final mandala value, as expressed in the actual physical body of the structure, came out to be 151'3½", the percentage of error in relationship to the Vastu unit of 2'9" would be 1.5%. If it can't be avoided, this is an acceptable margin of error. We could say that the frequency value of the mandala, as created by the physical structure expressing the perimeter value, remains in integrity.

However,

111 vitasti (vitasti = 1'4½") = 152'7½" perimeter value

If during construction the final mandala value, as expressed in the actual physical body of the structure, came out to be 152'8", the percentage of error in relationship to the Vastu unit of 1'4 ½" would be 3%, a less desirable margin of error but probably still acceptable.

225 taalam (taalam = 8 ¼") = 154'8¼" perimeter value

If during construction the final mandala value, as expressed in the actual physical body of the structure, came out to be 154'8¾", the percentage of error in relationship to the Vastu unit of 8¼"would be 6%, a much less desirable margin of error.

1333 angulas (angula = 1⅜") = 152'8⅞" perimeter value

If during construction, the final mandala value, as expressed in the actual physical body of the structure, came out to be 152'9⅜", the percentage of error in relationship to the Vastu unit of 1⅜"would be 36%, an undesirable margin of error.

This is not to say that the smaller Vastu units can't be used for building perimeters. It does mean that the demand on accuracy with the smaller units is exponentially higher.

Doors and entrance locations

One of the most significant factors in Vastu design is the location of the main formal entry door. This doorway should be the main entry for the owners at the front of the structure. (The front of the structure is considered to be the "facing direction." If the front of the structure is on the east side, then this is an east-facing structure.).

The diagram of the Paramasayika Mandala (the nine-by-nine grid pattern illustrated below) shows the location of the pada devatas and the general energetic effect on humans related to pada and entrance. Vastu science says that crossing the threshold at the center of a particular pada is a recognition and stimulation of the energy of that location.

Rule one is to locate the center of the main entry door of the structure at the center of a pada that has positive energy for humans. By "center of door," I mean the center of the active entry door, the center of the clear opening created by the single door used to enter the house. If you have a double or triple door, then you must place the center of the active door (the door you open to walk through) at the center of the pada. If you have a narrow double door and both activate when you enter, then place the center of the double doors at the center of the pada. (Refer to illustrations 17abc below.)

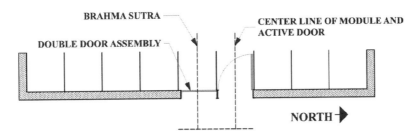

**Illustration 17a
Double door entry with center of active
door positioned in center of correct module**

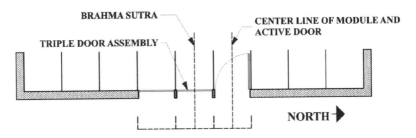

**Illustration 17b
Triple door entry with center of active
door positioned in center of correct module**

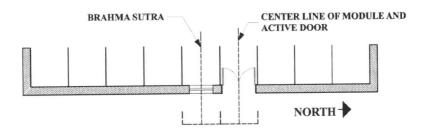

**Illustration 17c
Single door entry with two leaf door
assembly. Door positioned in center of
correct module**

The following mandala chart shows the location of auspicious entries on all sides of the structure. The chart indicates the predicted effect of an entry located at each particular module on the mandala. Obviously, we want to avoid entries where a negative influence is predicted. Nine padas are accepted as auspicious for "primary" entry of the structure: on the north, Soma, Bhallata and Mukhya Padas; on the east, Jayanta and Indra Padas; on the south, Gruhak Shata and Gandharva Padas; on the west, Sugriva and Pushpa Danta Padas. Centerline of main entry doors must be centered on one of these padas. No other primary entry door locations are accepted as auspicious for the Vastu structure.

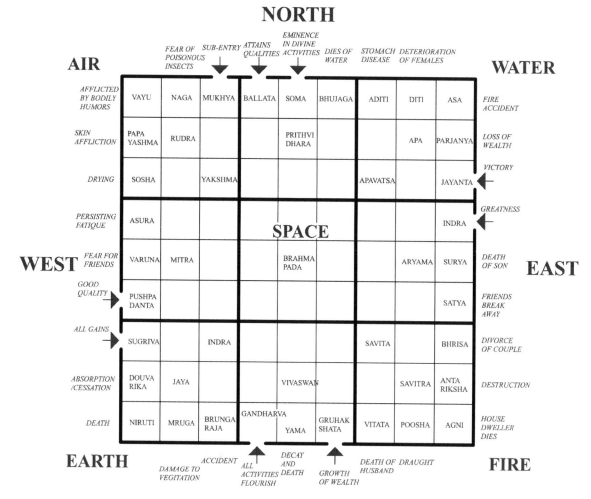

Illustration 18
Paramasaayika Vastu Purusha Mandala
with effects of entry locations
(Arrows indicate auspicious entry door locations)

Each point on the mandala perimeter has a particular type of energy that manifests an influence in the structure if it is activated by the ceremony of crossing over that pada with our body, attention, intention, and energy. When we cross the location, we are penetrating the sanctum of the house. We are coming into relationship with the house. Our energy and the energy of the house begin to comingle and influence each other. One might ask why negative effects would be present in certain locations. The explanation for negative influence is this: The energy is actually not good or bad, but it is too intense or inhuman for humans to flourish. For example, in the summer a gentle movement of air is soothing and refreshing. However, if we take the same element in nature—air—and we increase the energy to hurricane force, the air that was our "friend" is now our "enemy." It is the same air, but now it has a force or energy that is too strong for human comfort. In those locations on the VPM where entry is not recommended, the energy is too intense for positive result.

The VPM chart for entry presumes that the orientation of the mandala is in correct relationship to the cardinal points of the compass. In general, the mandala is aligned with north/south/east/west directions. A slight rotation of the structure is recommended; we will discuss this in another section.

In modern (especially Western) plan layouts, many times the homeowner will have a formal front door and a different "functional" entry door that is used most of the time. Usually the location of the functional entry door has a relationship with the street parking or garage area. Convenience and weather are the main influence for the location of this informal door.

In a structure where there is a need for a second primary entrance (an entrance from a garage location perhaps), the second primary door location must also be chosen from the list of nine primary door padas. For example, a house may have a main entry door facing the street in Indra Pada on the east but also have a second primary door leading from the garage to the Soma Pada on the north. The formal front door, however, is the most important one. This door should be the largest door in the house.

Light axes through the structure:

Once the main door is established in the floor plan, the designer should establish a clear line of sight through the structure to a window on the exterior wall on the opposite side of the house. This is called the "thread of light" in the house. I recommend that at least one half of the height of the front door is glass. This line of light is very important. It allows energy inside and outside the structure to move into and though the structure.

The thread of light is achieved by proper room and wall layouts and the use of doors and interior windows if necessary. If you use interior windows, the window width should be the same width as the front door or one half the width or three-fourths the width. If doors are used, the doors should have at least translucent glass in the upper part of the door. The general rule is to keep the centers of all openings aligned. The height of the window should be the same height as the front door.

The reason for this axial path through the structure is so that the house can breathe freely. It is said that this path is like a trachea (wind pipe) for the house. As we look down this line of sight, we should not see any columns or parts of walls obstructing. Also, no large tree trunks or boulders or body of water should sit directly outside the house on either end of this line of sight.

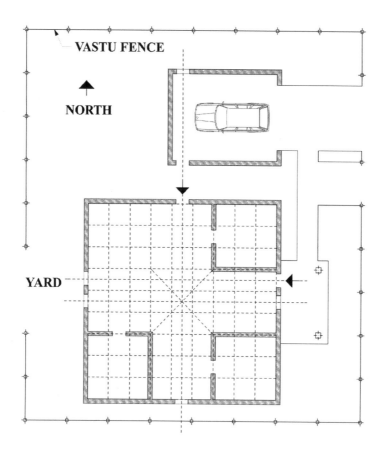

Illustration 19
Two doors in auspicous locations
for conditions where both doors
will be used often

The Vastu structure also requires two additional lines of light through the house: the Brahma Sutra and the Soma Sutra. The Brahma Sutra is the line of sight directly through the center of the VPM from the front of the house to the back. The Soma Sutra is the line of sight directly through the center of the VPM perpendicular to the Brahma Sutra. Brahma Sutra is always related to the facing direction of the house.

My experience in practical application of creating the three sutras in the structure is that it can be challenging in a modern structure, given the unique and complex programs of modern living. It is best to have all sutras honored on all floors. At the very least, you may have the thread of light and Brahma Sutra only, but this is not ideal.

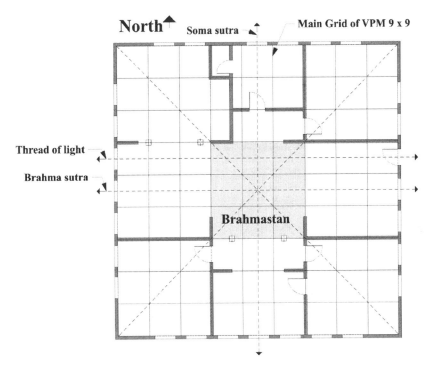

Illustration 20
Lines of light through the Vastu structure

The formal entry door should be used as often as possible by the owner. Conveniences aside, by making a commitment to live in a Vastu house in relationship with the living structure and in relationship with all the positive cosmic influences it enlivens, the owner needs to exercise the choice to activate the positive energy available entering and exiting at the formal front door.

Living in a Vastu residence gives us the opportunity to live with respect for nature and cosmic energy. When living in such a structure, we are not merely sheltering in a comfortable, beautiful structure; we are living in conscious relationship with cosmic energy. This conscious relationship requires a certain formality or respect in terms of how we live in the structure. Dwelling in these structures can become a constant celebration of life, an act of gratitude and an honoring of laws of nature. Also, our own inner nature is being honored and uplifted by our relationship with the structure.

Entry door and sutra lines in relationship to Vastu compound wall:
The Vastu wall around the house should have an opening in the form of a window in centerline relationship to the entry door line of site and also the Brahma Sutra and Soma Sutra lines. If the fence is low, below 3'- 0", this opening is not required because a line of site can extend over the wall without obstruction.

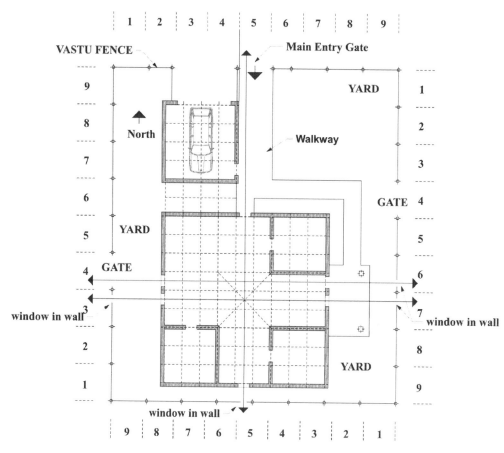

Illustration 21
Openings in Vastu fence
opposite lines of light through the
structure

Secondary exterior doors:

Secondary doors (doors not used as primary entrance) on an exterior wall that fall on the VPM perimeter are allowed in specific padas. Secondary doors must also be centered in the pada.

Three rules determine the location of secondary doors:

1) The primary entry door locations listed above can also serve as secondary door locations.

2) Added to this list are eight additional padas that are accepted for secondary door location, on the north, Naga and Diti Padas; on the east, Bhrisa Pada; on the south, Vitata and Brunga Raja Padas; on the west, Douva Rika and Sosha Padas.

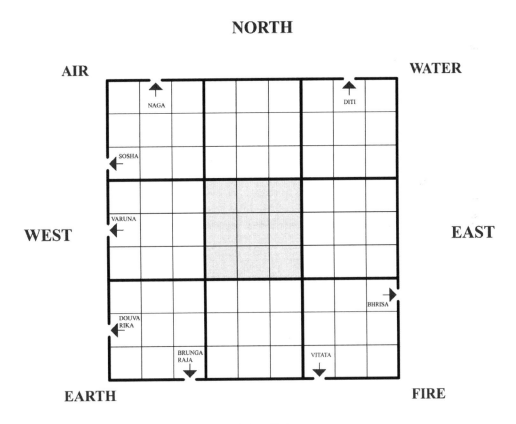

Illustration 22
Vastu Purusha Mandala with secondary
exterior door locations
(Not for use as a main entry door)

3) A secondary door may be located directly opposite the primary entry door on the other side of the house, with the exception of the center south pada. A center south pada should never be used for an entry door, primary or secondary.

Doors in extensions:

If the structure has extensions from the mandala with doors in the exterior walls of the extension, the doors must be placed in direct relationship to the accepted entry location on the related mandala perimeter.

Illustration 23
Alignment of entry door in extension area
with correct mandala entry location on
main wall of Vastu Purusha Mandala

Interior doors:

In a simple house with few walls, interior doors should align with the exterior openings (windows or doors) of the house. In a complex, modern floor plan, interior doors offer some challenges. Door locations need to make sense in terms of room function, or activity in the house will be disrupted on a practical level. The important axial lines in the house—thread of light from front door, Brahma Sutra, and Soma Sutra—need to be honored; but other than that, interior doors can be placed in practical locations as needed.

Door swing direction:

When possible, have the swing of the door move in a clockwise direction. This is a general rule to be applied when possible, but it can be ignored at times due to practical considerations.

Window locations in exterior walls:

Windows in exterior walls are to be located in relationship to the mandala pada (module). Windows shall be centered on pada when possible. This is the ideal relationship of window to Vastu Purusha Mandala. Double windows are centered in module; triple windows are centered in module, etc. Ideally there are no windows in the corner modules. However, in practice, it is sometimes necessary to place windows in the corner areas for practical reasons. If this is done, always keep a post at the exact corner. Do not create a window that has glass through the corner of the Vastu Purusha Mandala. *[See illustration on next page.]*

Ayadi for doors and windows:

Ayadi calculations can be applied to doors and windows. At least the front door, if possible, should take on an Ayadi value. To create a door with correct Ayadi value, we usually use a unit dimension of 8¼", 1⅜", or 13/64" and consider the perimeter of the *clear opening*, not the door dimension or window dimension. Usually the door or window is slightly larger than the clear opening due to the material used to stop the door when it closes. For example, a door may be 3'0" wide and 6'8" high, but the clear opening when the door is not closed is perhaps ½" smaller in width and height.

Ratio of width to height is also considered when constructing an opening for a door or window. The width to height ratio should be increments of 1:1, 1:1.25, 1:1.5, 1:1.75, and 1:2. Alternatively, the ratio could be 1:1.12 5, 1:1.375, 1:1.625, 1:1.875.

If it is cost prohibitive to give an Ayadi value to doors and windows, this refinement can be set aside.

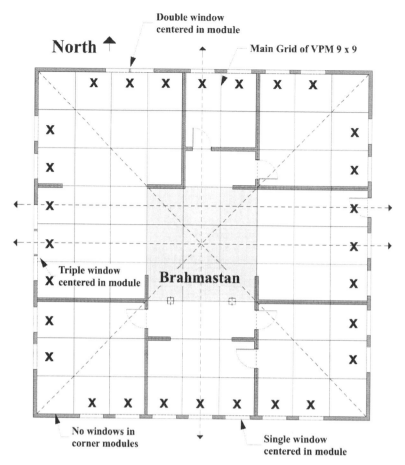

Illustration 24
Window locations on Exterior Walls
"x" indicates modules (padas) where
windows can be placed

Resonance with VPM: wall location

How does the structure gain resonance with the Vastu Purusha Mandala and therefore with cosmic and Earth energies? The architect first chooses and draws out the VPM with all correct measurement values. For example,

1) The unit value being used is the hasta (2'9").

2) The mandala perimeter value is chosen in regard to all good influences, taking into consideration the occupants of the building, the orientation of the building, the desired square footage of the building, etc. For our example we will choose 55 hastas = 151'3" perimeter value.

3) The chosen ratio of one side to its perpendicular side will be 1:1, a square mandala.

4) The VPM is created by drawing the nine-by-nine grid with correct perimeter values of 37'9¾" on each side and equaling a total perimeter value of 151'3."

5) The module of the VPM is determined to be 4'2 13/32" x 4'2 13/32". (37'9¾" ÷ 9 = 4'2 13/32"). The VPM has eighty-one such modules.

At this point the architect has the basic geometric foundation of the entire house. All walls are to be in relationship to the grid lines of the VPM.

6) The wall layout can proceed by setting the exterior walls to a consistent relationship to the perimeter lines of the VPM. Three choices of relationship to the mandala grid line for the exterior walls are possible:

A) inside finished face of wall on grid line

B) outside finished face of wall on grid line

C) center of wall on grid line

Maintain a consistent relationship of exterior walls to grid line. For example, if the chosen relationship is inside face of wall on grid line, then all exterior walls must have that relationship.

If *outside face* of wall is used, it is important to have the exact dimension of the wall thickness in resonance with the module of the grid. In center of wall and inside face of wall relationships, wall thickness is not critical. However, if it is possible within the scope of the project to create a wall that has a thickness related to the module, it is good to take the opportunity. (Please refer to the section on wall thickness for how to do this.)

The ideal relationship for interior walls is center of wall on grid line. However, it is accepted that interior walls can also have finished face of wall on grid line. Ideally the architect chooses a consistent relationship to the grid line. It is best not to have a constantly changing relationship of wall to grid line.

Defining "finished face of wall": The finished face of wall is the final surface of the wall, not including any trim detail at the top or bottom of the wall. Examples of finished face of wall:

A) Brick and mortar with plaster veneer: the finished face of plaster veneer is the finished face of wall. The rough face of brick should not be used as a Vastu dimension point.

B) Wood framing with gypsum board wall sheathing, a very thin layer of sheathing joint plaster and paint: The face of gypsum board would be considered the Vastu dimension point. In typical gypsum board construction, the coat of fine plaster placed on the wall to cover the joints is usually thin enough to be ignored. However, if there is going to be a significant layer of plaster over gypsum board (more than ⅛") the Vastu architect will review this condition with the builder and adjust the dimensions if necessary.

C) Straw bale or adobe with mud plaster, rough and finish coats: The face of finished clay plaster coat would be the Vastu dimension point.

D) Wooden log wall (no interior sheathing): The face of log wall would be the Vastu dimension point. If the log is round faced, it is not an ideal condition, but the thickest part of the log would most likely set the dimension. The Vastu architect should review the condition.

The Brahmastan of the structure is the center nine modules of the eight-one module VPM. No wall construction should take place within the Brahmastan. However, walls can be located around the perimeter of the Brahmastan, following the proper relationship of grid line to wall.

In general, the exercise is to place the walls of the structure in direct relationship to the underlying grid lines of the VPM. The most ideal Vastu floor plan uses only the main nine-by-nine Vastu Purusha Mandala lines for the wall layout, using only a few walls to delineate rooms where necessary. Simple plans are the best, in my opinion.

If the floor plan includes columns, all columns should be located such that the center of column lands on a crossing point of the VPM grid. However, as with wall, no columns shall be located within the Brahmastan.

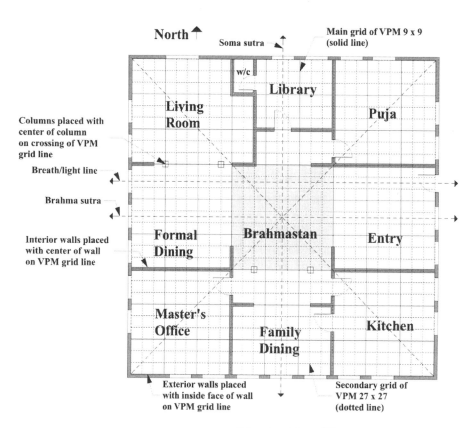

Illustration 25
Sample floor plan showing how walls relate
to the Vastu Purusha Mandala

Plan "extensions":

The ideal Vastu structure will not place energetically polluting elements, stairs, bathrooms, or toilets, within the Vastu Purusha Mandala. The ideal locations for these elements are in "extension" areas outside the VPM. (The ideal location for polluting elements is discussed later in this text).

The extension area can be attached to the VPM and under the same roof structure. Extensions follow the grid pattern of the VPM. They can expand outward from one to three modules from the VPM. Expansion needs to begin one module inside the corner of the VPM. Extensions can house other functions also, such as bedrooms and living rooms and a general use room related to the functional prescriptions for the side of the mandala where the extension is. Ideally we keep the main prescribed functions within the VPM. For example, the kitchen should be within the southeast corner of the VPM, not in an extension to the south or east. The master bedroom sleeping area is ideally located within the southwest area of the VPM. The puja, or meditation room, is located within the northeast area of the VPM. Use the following illustration as a guide to create extensions in the floor plan.

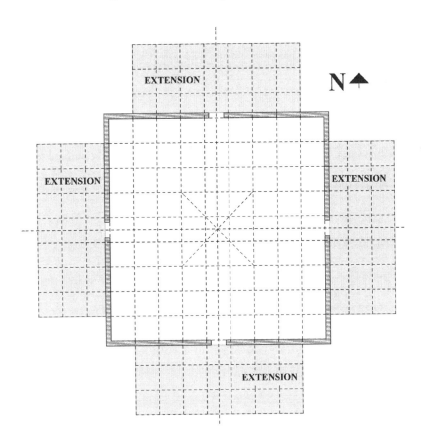

Illustration 26
Extensions allowed to the
Vastu Purusha Mandala

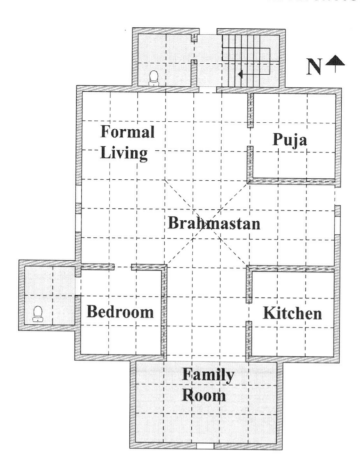

Illustration 27
Example of using extensions
to add space to a floor plan

Prescribed plan patterns and proportions

Vastu architecture prescribes specific shapes for the floor plan of a structure. The basic plan patterns are square (Chaturmuka Griham), rectangular (Dandaka Griham), L-shaped (Laangala Griham), and U-shaped (Moulika Griham).

The square (Chaturmuka Griham) or rectangular (Dandaka Griham) plan pattern can be oriented to north, south, east, or west. The Brahmastan comprises the center nine modules of the structure.

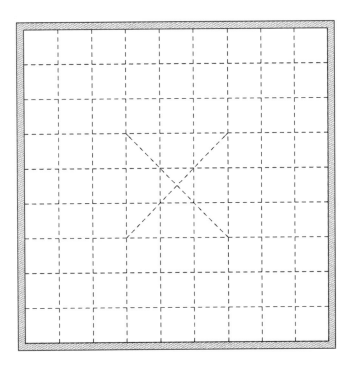

Illustration 28
Square pattern
Chaturmuka Griham

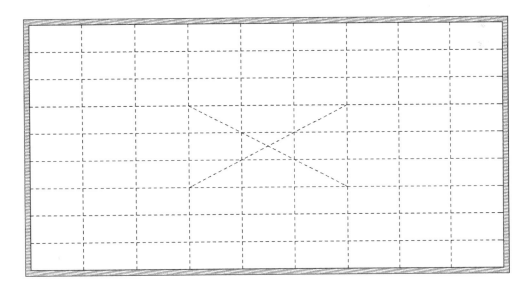

Illustration 29
Rectangular pattern
Dandaka Griham

The L-shape plan pattern allows for the Brahmastan to fall outside of the interior space of the structure. This pattern has an orientation restriction: the only orientation allowed is for interior structure to be placed in the west and south areas of the mandala, as illustrated. The Brahmastan comprises the center nine modules, which are in part of the open courtyard of the structure. This structure requires at least a low wall to finish the mandala perimeter on the north and east sides, with gate entries located appropriately with respect to prescribed VPM locations and orientation.

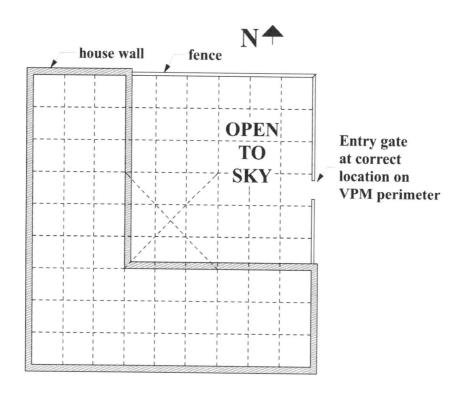

Illustration 30
"L" shaped pattern
Laangala Griham

The U-shape plan pattern allows for the Brahmastan to fall outside the interior space of the structure. The pattern also has an orientation restriction: the open section can only be on the north or east side of the structure as illustrated. The Brahmastan comprises the center nine modules, which are in part of the open courtyard of the structure. This structure also requires at least a low wall to finish the mandala perimeter on the north or east sides, with gate entries located appropriately with respect to prescribed VPM locations and orientation.

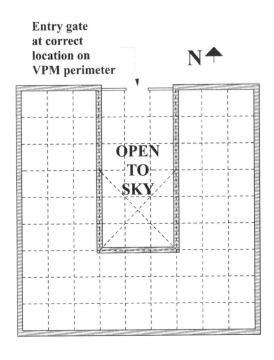

**Illustration 31
"U" shaped pattern
Moulika Griham**

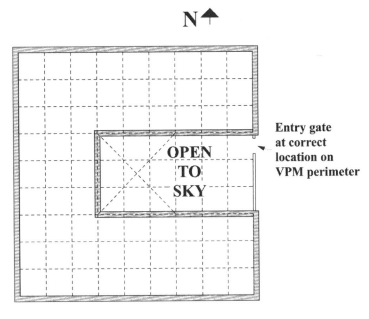

**Illustration 32
"U" shaped pattern
Moulika Griham**

The square or rectangular plan with the center open to sky is a classic pattern in South India. This plan can be oriented to north, south, east, or west. The Brahmastan comprises the center nine modules, which are in the open courtyard of the structure.

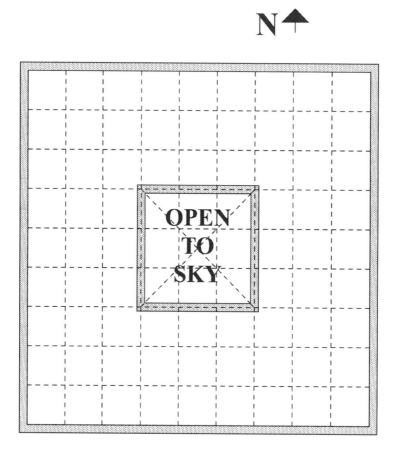

Illustration 33
Square pattern
with center open to sky

Rectangular Vastu Purusha Mandala must follow specific proportions of width to length. The prescribed proportions are 1:1.25, 1:1.50, 1:1.75 and 1:2.00. It does not matter whether the width or length is the eastern face of the structure.

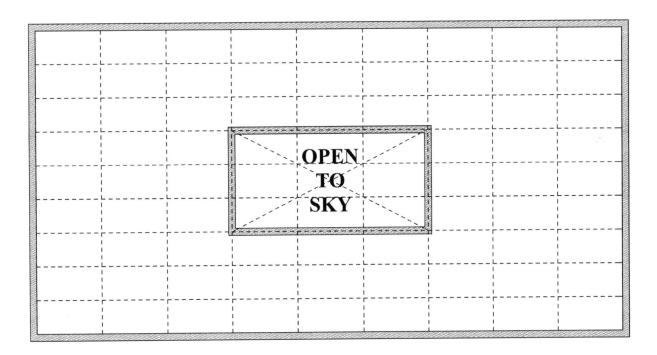

Illustration 34
Rectangular pattern
with center open to sky

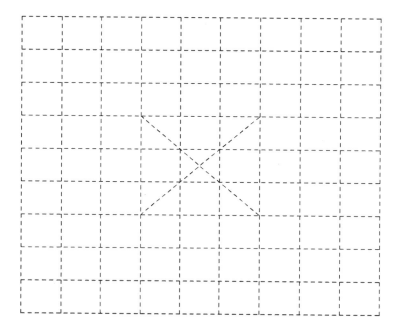

Illustration 34a
Rectangular proportion 1:1.25

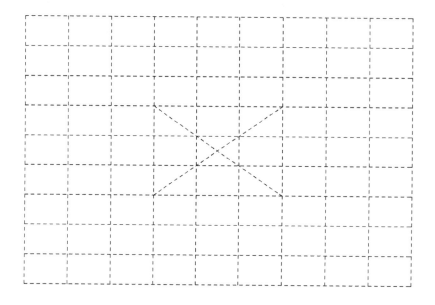

Illustration 34b
Rectangular proportion 1:1.50

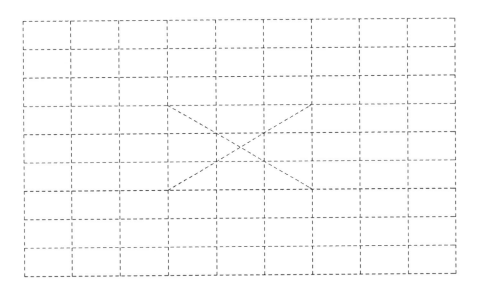

Illustration 34c
Rectangular proportion 1:1.75

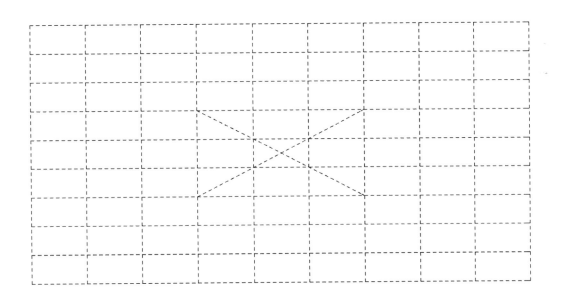

Illustration 34d
Rectangular proportion 1:2.00

Plan extensions and the different mandala patterns:

Once the Vastu Purusha Mandala pattern geometry has been established, the design can add extensions as discussed above. Below are some examples of patterns with extensions.

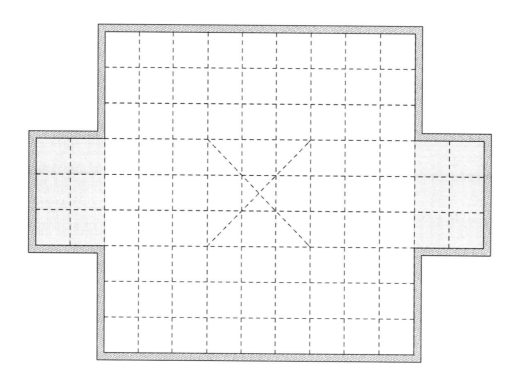

Illustration 35
Chaturmuka Griham pattern
with extensions

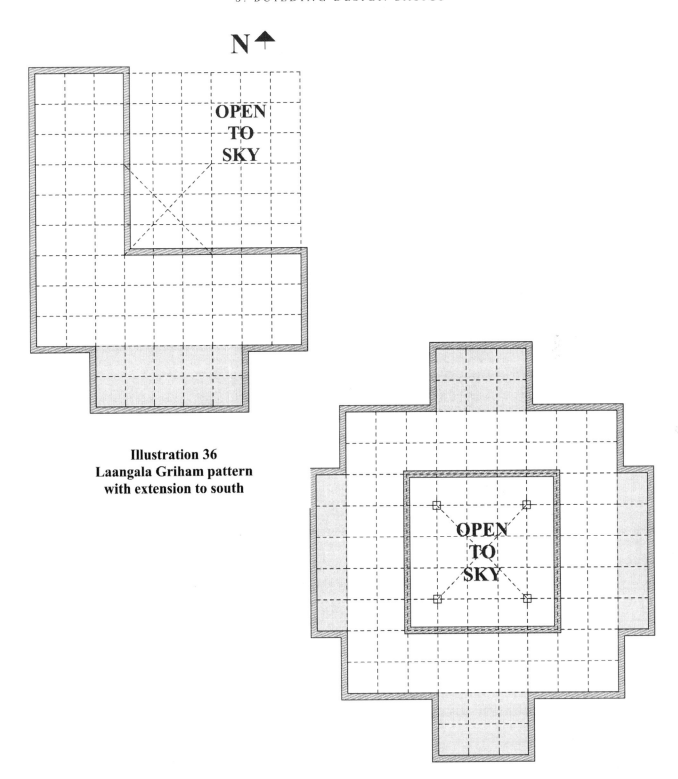

N↑

OPEN
TO
SKY

Illustration 36
Laangala Griham pattern
with extension to south

OPEN
TO
SKY

Illustration 37
Central courtyard pattern
with extensions

An ideal pattern:

The open-to-sky courtyard with a surrounding walkway is an ideal pattern for a Vastu structure.

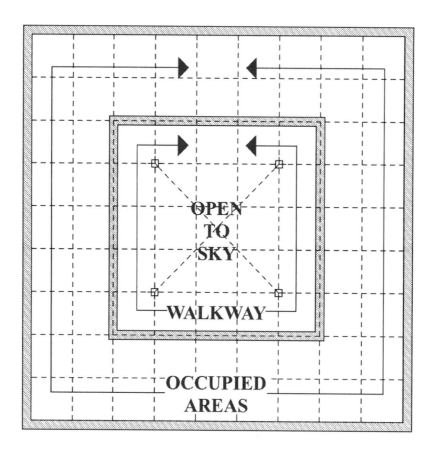

Illustration 38
An ideal pattern for a Vastu residence

Curved or diagonal walls in the floor plan:

The VPM is a mandala with an orthogonal mandate. The lines of the mandala run parallel and perpendicular to each other. As explained earlier this "checkerboard" mandala is the expression of nature's embryonic pattern of manifestation from formless energy into matter. Therefore, the walls of a Vastu structure, if they are to remain resonant and in harmony with the VPM, must remain in direct relationship to the mandala pattern. Curved and diagonal walls create dissonant space and energy within a Vastu structure. They are not recommended.

With the direct guidance of a Vastu architect, it is sometimes possible to use curved or diagonal forms in extensions of the VPM, as illustrated below. However, these elements should only be employed with guidance.

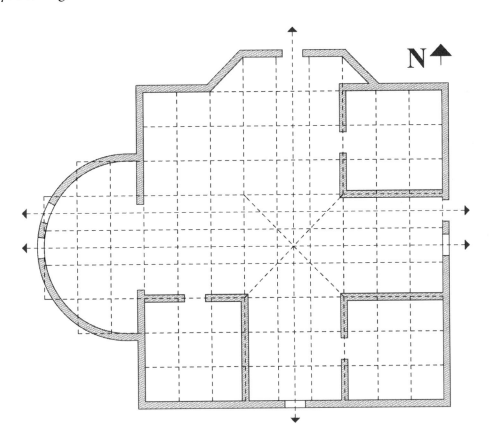

Illustration 39
Example of the use of circular
and diagonal elements outside the
Vastu Purusha Mandala
(sometimes allowed with professional
guidance)

Wall thickness

Wall thickness is defined as face of finished wall to face of finished wall, (including veneer plasters, wood, etc.). There are ideal conditions and acceptable conditions for wall thicknesses.

Ideal conditions:
Wall thickness can be an expression of a fraction of the module of the nine-by-nine VPM. Wall thickness can be multiples of 1/9 or 1/27 of the module. For example, if the VPM is 175'6", then the module is 4'10½"; therefore, the wall thickness can be 1/9 = 6½" or 2/27 = 4 11/32 or 2/9 = 13" or 7/27 = 15 5/32", and so forth.

This fractional relationship with the module of the VPM keeps the walls in resonance with it.

Acceptable conditions:

In modern building conditions, wall thicknesses are often fixed by standard constructions, using standard materials. The Vastu designer may not have the option to reset the wall size to be in resonance with a chosen module. In this situation it is acceptable to use standard wall thickness (with one exception to be explained below). Standard walls are to be placed in relationship to the VPM gridlines in as consistent a relationship as possible. All exterior walls should maintain the same relationship to the perimeter grid line of the VPM: inside face of wall on grid line or center of wall on grid line (either of these two is acceptable for standard wall constructions).

The one restriction for exterior walls is this: If you place the *outside face of wall* on the VPM perimeter grid line, then you must adjust the wall thickness for resonance with the module of the VPM. For example, if the VPM module is 4'10½", then the exterior wall thickness must be a multiple of 1/9 or 1/27 of the module. In this example it could be 1/9 = 6½" or 2/27 = 4 11/32" or 2/9 = 13"or 7/27 = 15 5/32", and so forth.

Enclosing Vastu fence

Every Vastu building should have an enclosing fence around it. This fence acts as a container for the energy of the building. If the fence is not surrounding the building, its energy will tend to dissipate out into the landscape.

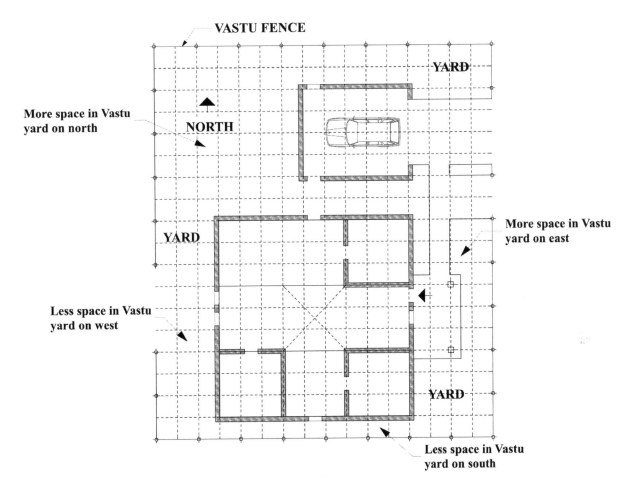

VASTU FENCE

YARD

More space in Vastu
yard on north

NORTH

More space in Vastu
yard on east

YARD

Less space in Vastu
yard on west

YARD

Less space in Vastu
yard on south

**Illustration 40
Example of a Vastu fence
layout**

Rules for the Vastu fence:

1) The fence falls on the grid lines of the mandala extended into the land surrounding the house. The fence should have the same relationship to the grid lines as the house walls do, but choose one and stick with it for the whole fence layout:

    a) inside face of wall on grid line

    b) outside face of wall on grid line

    c) center of wall on grid line

2) When creating the walled compound around the house with the fence, the distance from the building to the fence should be greater on the north and east sides than on the south and west sides.

3) The main entry to the Vastu compound should be located by:

A) Dividing the length of the fence on the chosen side into nine modules

B) Centering the gate opening on that side in an auspicious module, according to the mandala requirements of the orientation, north, south, east, or west.

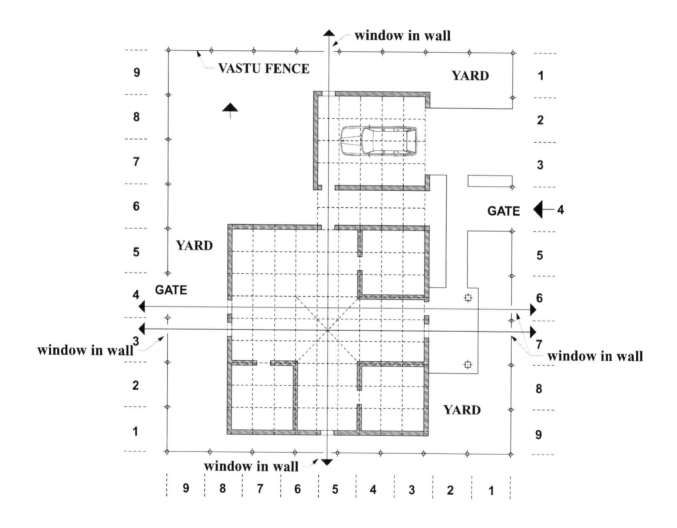

Illustration 41
Example of how to locate entry
gates for the Vastu

The main entry gate can be on one side of the plot, and the main entry door to the building can be on another. The main consideration is to select the entry gate location with respect to prescribed module locations. See below for an east-facing structure with a north-facing entry gate.

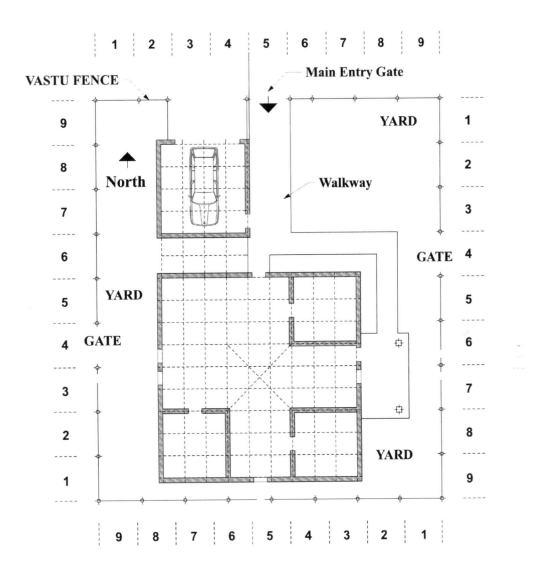

Illustration 42
Example of a north entry gate
and east facing house

4) The designer must extend the central axis lines of the structure running east/west and north/south to the Vastu fence in both directions and the line running from the center of the front entry door to the back of the house. If the Vastu wall is solid and tall, there should be a window or opening in the wall centered on that extended axis line. This opening is not a gate; it is a "window" in the wall to allow these lines of sight to pass unobstructed through the compound. If the Vastu wall is a low construction (below the navel), an opening in the wall isn't necessary.

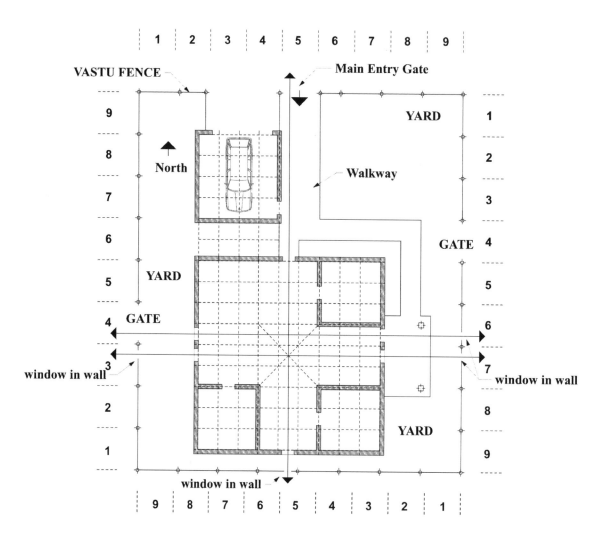

Illustration 43
Example of openings located in
Vastu fence opposite lines of
sight through the structure

Practical construction considerations

Some general notes for prospective builders and homeowners:

1) The dimensions of the house, as dictated by the Vastu Purusha Mandala given by the Vastu architect are *very* important. When followed precisely, they allow the house to have a geometry and proportion that is resonant with healing and nurturing earthly and cosmic energies. The project architect *must* insist from the beginning with all contractors that the Vastu project is extremely demanding with regard to the dimensions. All dimensions are to be followed exactly, and the project architect and builder are responsible for verifying the dimensions and calling for corrections if they are needed.

On the other hand, construction materials can be inconsistent in dimension and stability. The general protocol is for the construction professional to measure and build to the precise dimensions called for by the Vastu architect; but maintaining the stability of dimensions may be challenging. Depending on weather conditions and other factors, dimensions can change slightly. The constructor's first job always is to measure and verify that the dimensions are in integrity; the constructor must check the dimensions throughout the construction period and make corrections if significant changes have occurred. This will eliminate most dimensional problems and the building will come very close to the prescribed conditions.

2) A surveyor is necessary to site the house with the proper orientation. The surveyor must give the layout lines before the foundation is excavated, and these lines shall maintain their integrity for verifying the orientation throughout the project.

3) The project architect or project contractor shall be responsible for the correctness of building orientation and verify it with a professional surveyor A) before excavation, B) after foundation forming and before the concrete is placed in the forms, and C) after the concrete forms are stripped and before the construction of the walls.

Protocol for checking dimensions:
Check all dimensions:

1) After the foundation is formed and before concrete for the foundation is poured.

2) After the foundation concrete is set and stripped of its forms. At this time the contractor can determine if the wall layout requires any corrections to get back to correct dimensions.

3) During the wall construction, the contractor and architect shall check dimensions and make sure the constructors are honoring the layout.

The object of these protocols is to have the goal of honoring the dimensions at all times to the 1/16" (1.5mm). The measuring device has these small dimension indicators, and a pencil mark can be made to these marks.

With all types of construction, the dimensions will be slightly off perfection and may even change during construction due to weather and material properties. If the builder honors the dimension every time he/she measures a layout, then the discrepancies will be kept to a minimum. Any discrepancies shall be reported to the client and the Vastu designer as soon as they have been identified.

Room layout according to function

Once the structure is placed on the ground in relationship to a VPM, which is aligned with true north/south/east/west, it comes under the influence of earthly and cosmic energies. These energies are gross and subtle. The correct placement on the Earth allows for the structure to vibrate in harmony with it. By creating a structured space that is related to a Vastu grid and placing it on the ground in correct orientation, the space can come into harmony with the earth grid. Resonance with the Earth grid gives the structure the ability to resonate with the macroscopic structure of the solar grid and the galactic grid and the universal grid, and it begins to vibrate with life-enhancing energy, coming alive.

Note: The Vastu-prescribed room placements with respect to the location within the VPM are universally applied in both the Northern and Southern Hemispheres.

The VPM of the structure is divided into nine equal parts. The center ninth of the VPM, the Brahmastan, is the heart of the house. The building, vibrating in resonance with the universe matrix and the earth matrix, is flooded with energy at the Brahmastan. Enclosed space in the structure is not empty space; a luminous, subtle substance fills this space. This sympathetic response, this vibration energy at the core of the building, is a process of manifestation from subtle to gross. As the energy moves from subtle (pure energy) to gross (material form), it begins to take on attributes. Attributes (elements) begin to manifest and gather in a prescribed arrangement. In the Brahmastan the subtle space element manifests. From the center the energy spreads out to the corners of the VPM. Each of the four gross elements, Fire, Earth, Air, and Water, manifest in designated areas: Fire (Agni), southeast; Earth (Nirruti), southwest; Air (Vayu), northwest; Water (Esana), northeast.

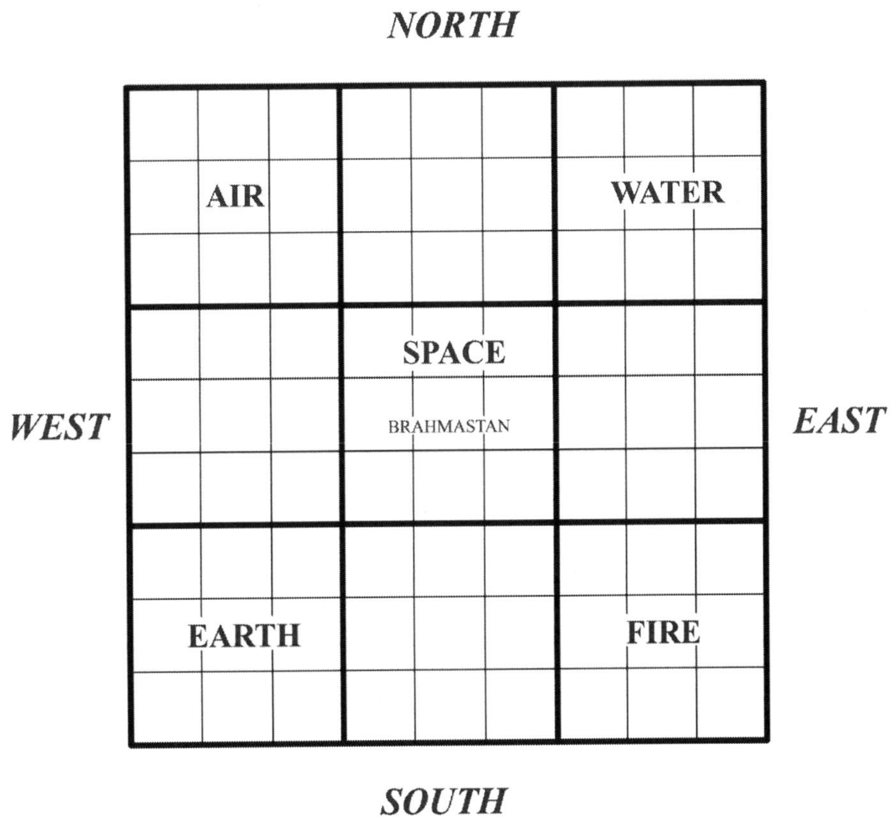

NORTH

```
                  AIR                    WATER



WEST                    SPACE                        EAST

                     BRAHMASTAN



                 EARTH                   FIRE


```

SOUTH

Illustration 44
VASTU PURUSHA MANDALA

Each area of the VPM has prescribed recommended functions relating to the element influence found there:

Southeast

The southeast is under the influence of the Fire (Agni) element, which is heat that activates energy. This area of the VPM is the traditional place for cooking food. The cook should *face east while cooking* at a counter on the east wall. The stovetop cooking is best located in the second pada from the southeast corner on the east wall: Anta Riksha. Cooking done in this location while facing east has a very beneficial influence for the mistress of the house. The luminary of this pada affects the nervous system of the person while near the pada. The effect is to stimulate righteousness and right action, action in accord with the laws of nature.

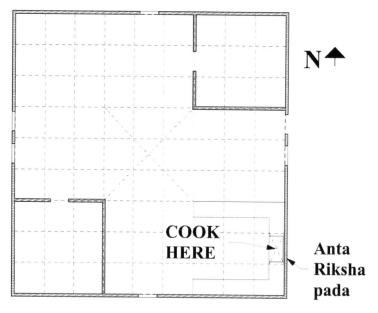

Illustration 45
Ideal location for cooking

The southeast area can also be used for the following part-time functions (meaning occupants should not expect to spend long periods of time there):
- Study area
- Office
- Machinery area
- Mechanical room/heating
- Informal kitchen dining
- Bedroom for short term guests
- Gym

Southeast area is the best place for a fireplace.

Functions that should not be in southeast area within the VPM:
- Puja or meditation area
- Bedroom
- Multi-hour office
- Water tank
- Toilet or bathing area (some exceptions could apply as directed by a Vastu consultant)
- Stairs
- Laundry (some exceptions could apply as directed by a Vastu consultant)
- Treasury

Southwest

The southwest corner of the VPM is under the influence of the Earth (Nirruti) element. The influence of this element is heaviness, calmness, coolness. It is a good location for the master of the house to have the bedroom. Also, it is a good location for the husband or wife of the house to have an office.

The southwest area can also be used for the following:
- Living or family room
- Bedroom
- Library
- Secondary location for meditation room
- Gym

Functions that should not be in southwest area within the VPM:
- Kitchen
- Toilet or bathing area (some exceptions could apply as directed by a Vastu consultant)
- Fireplace (If located *outside* the Vastu Purusha Mandala, it might be allowed.)
- Stairs
- Heating facility
- Laundry

Northwest

The northwest corner of the VPM is under the influence of the Air (Vayu) element. The influence of this element is movement. In traditional Vastu homes in India, the northwest area is used for a storeroom. The influence of "movement" brings about a transition of materials in this area. Things move in and out. However, this area can be used for many purposes.

The northwest area can also be used for the following:
- Bedroom—best for young adult nearing an age when they will be moving out
- Guest room
- Living or family room
- Office (except if used full time)
- Library
- Second choice for heating/mechanical room
- Second choice for kitchen—not usually recommended
- Gym

Northwest area is a place to put a fireplace, if properly placed by a Vastu architect.

Functions that should not be in northwest area within the VPM:

- Toilet or bathing area (some exceptions could apply as directed by a Vastu consultant)
- Stairs
- Bedroom for young child
- Bedroom for master or mistress of house
- Treasury
- Home office that is used many hours a day

Northeast

The northeast corner of the VPM is under the influence of the water (Esana) element. The water element influence is fertility and power. Puja and meditation rooms are best located in this area.

The northeast area can also be used for the following:

- Office for master or mistress of the house
- Bedroom for elders
- Bedroom for monk
- Under specific circumstances it could be an extension of a living or family room.
- Library or study
- Water tank (on the roof, for example)
- Bedroom for family member as directed by an expert Vastu consultant

Functions that should not be in northeast area within the VPM:
- Toilet or bathing area
- Stairs
- Fireplace
- Kitchen
- Heating/mechanical room
- Gym
- Guest bedroom, unless for older people
- Septic tank or waste water storage

In the Vastu Shastras, it is mentioned that bathing rooms can be in the east or north side of the building; however, no mention is made of installing a toilet in those areas. In general toilets are considered to be polluting elements and are best kept outside the area of the VPM in certain designated locations to be illustrated later in this text. In practice I find that bathing areas can be in the west and south also, if properly located.

3. BUILDING DESIGN BASICS

The next zones of the VPM to be considered are the intermediate zones between the corners: middle of east, south, west, and north.

East/Middle (between northeast and southeast)

The middle of the eastern part is the area of the VPM where the Indra energy is located. Functions that are good for this area:
- Ladies area: office or resting room for ladies
- Living/family room
- If main entry door is in the east, then an entry hall or waiting room is allowed
- Dining area
- Bedroom
- Office/library
- Meeting room

South/Middle (between southwest and southeast)

The middle southern part is the area of the VPM where the Yama energy is located. Functions that are good for this area:
- Bedroom (bedroom for the owner of the house can also be here)
- Dining
- Living/family room
- Kitchen—*non-cooking* area
- Office/library

West/Middle (between northwest and southwest)

The middle western part is the area of the VPM where the Varuna energy is located. Functions that are good for this area:
- Dining area
- Bedroom
- Living/family room
- Office/library

North/Middle (between northeast and northwest)

The middle north is the area of the VPM where the Kubera energy is located. Functions that are good for this area:
- Treasury
- Bedroom
- Living/family room
- Office/library

As stated above the center section of the VPM, as defined by the center nine modules of the eighty-one module VPM is the Brahmastan. This area is the location of Brahma (Shiva) energy. It must be free of columns and walls. In a traditional Vastu house of Tamil Nadu, the Brahmastan is an open-to-sky courtyard. This is considered the ideal pattern for a Vastu structure: to have the center open to rain and sun, moon and star light. *In modern houses this area can have a roof over it as long as there is light coming in from above from clerestory walls or a substantial skylight.*

Brahmastan should be honored on all floors of the structure, including the basement and attic area. However, there is no need to create an open shaft from the top floor to the basement for light from above. As long as the roof has some skylight or clerestory opening to the top habitable floor, the need for the influence of light for the Brahmastan is fulfilled.

Brahmastan is the sacred center of the structure. It is the reason we want to live in such a structure. The Vastu energy materializes in that area and spreads outward through the structure. Its function is to energize the structure. We need not desire any other function for it. The centrality of this area means the occupants walk through it to reach other areas of the structure. Also, the area can be used for short term activities of celebration and gathering. It can be incorporated as part of a larger family room area, but it should be honored and occupied in a way that gives attention to its geometry. The very center of the Brahmastan should be kept clear of fixed objects, such as furniture.

In general each floor should stay at the same level in a Vastu house. The floor plan should not contain raised and sunken areas. However, the Brahmastan area can be depressed slightly if desired.

In the construction of the Vastu structure, installation of the mechanical systems, such as heating, ventilating, cooling, electrical supply, plumbing supply, plumbing waste, and communication services, shall not encroach upon the Brahmastan. None of these mechanical systems can run through the Brahmastan. However, these systems can run up to and around the perimeter of the Brahmastan. It is OK to have a few light fixtures and/or a ceiling fan in the Brahmastan area.

Functions that should not be in the Brahmastan area:
- Toilet or bathing area
- Stairs
- Fireplace
- Kitchen
- Heating/mechanical room
- Gym
- Sleeping area
- Office
- Treasury
- Dining

Note: *Orientation of the bed* is prescribed in Vastu architecture. The correct orientation of the bed is to have the top of the bed (the "top" being where the head of the sleeper is) to the east or south. This means that when lying down to sleep the top of the head is to the east or south.

Location of polluting elements in the floor plan

Bathrooms, toilets and stairs:

Toilet areas and stairs are considered to create a polluting influence from the point of view of energy. Ideally these functional elements are placed outside the mandala geometry in an extension of the mandala. Also, it is best if they do not line up with extensions of the center line of the VPM (north to south and east of west) in both directions or the diagonal lines (northeast to southwest and southeast to northwest) of the VPM.

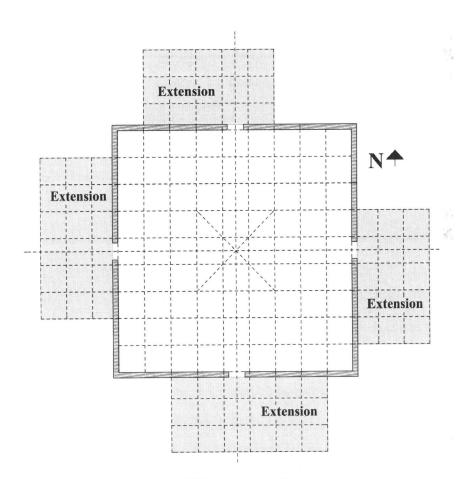

Illustration 46
Extension areas outside the VPM
where polluting elements can be located

If is it necessary to place a bathroom or toilet *within* the mandala, certain zones can be utilized. The basic goal is to keep these elements out of the corner areas (especially the northeast and southwest corners), off the central axes, and out of the Brahmastan.

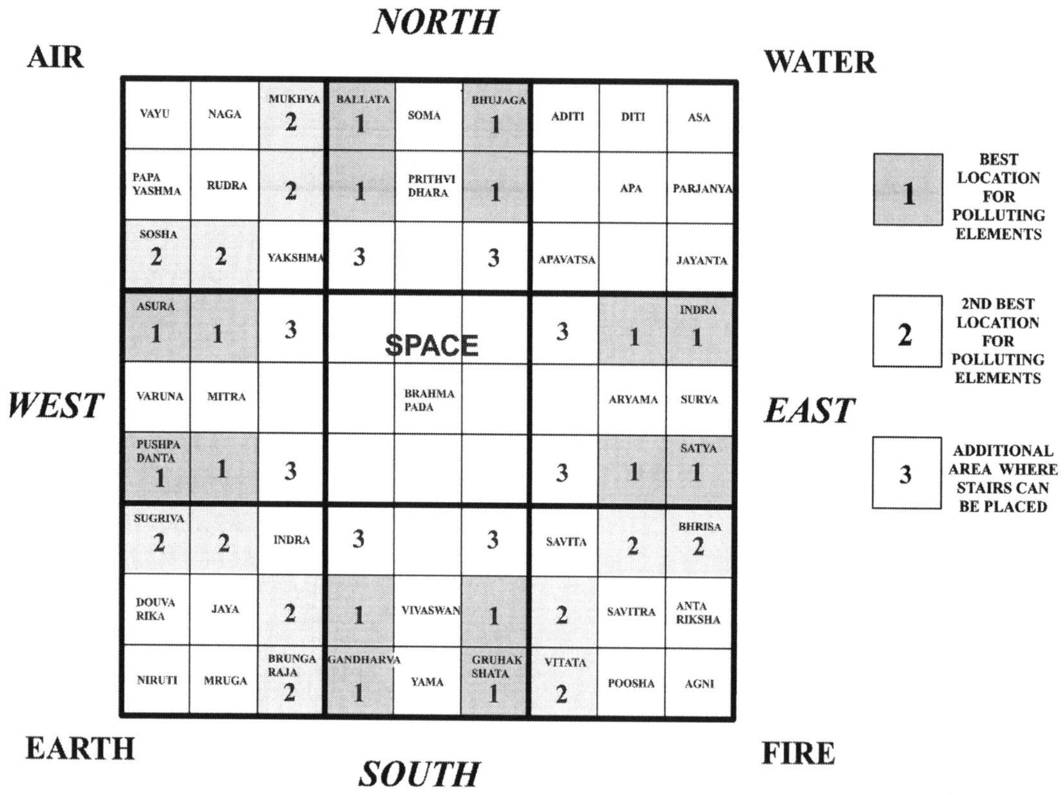

NORTH

AIR　　　　　　　　　　　　　　　　　　**WATER**

VAYU	NAGA	MUKHYA 2	BALLATA 1	SOMA	BHUJAGA 1	ADITI	DITI	ASA
PAPA YASHMA	RUDRA	2	1	PRITHVI DHARA	1		APA	PARJANYA
SOSHA 2	2	YAKSHMA	3		3	APAVATSA		JAYANTA
ASURA 1	1	3	SPACE		3	1		INDRA 1
VARUNA	MITRA		BRAHMA PADA			ARYAMA	SURYA
PUSHPA DANTA 1	1	3			3	1	SATYA 1
SUGRIVA 2	2	INDRA	3		3	SAVITA	2	BHRISA 2
DOUVA RIKA	JAYA	2	1	VIVASWAN	1	2	SAVITRA	ANTA RIKSHA
NIRUTI	MRUGA	BRUNGA RAJA 2	GANDHARVA 1	YAMA	GRUHAK SHATA 1	VITATA 2	POOSHA	AGNI

WEST　　　　　　　　　　　　　　　　　　**EAST**

1	BEST LOCATION FOR POLLUTING ELEMENTS
2	2ND BEST LOCATION FOR POLLUTING ELEMENTS
3	ADDITIONAL AREA WHERE STAIRS CAN BE PLACED

EARTH　　　　　　　　　　　　　　　　　　**FIRE**

SOUTH

Illustration 47
Zones for toilets and stairs
within the VPM

Acceptable orientation for a toilet is to have the fixture aligned north to south, with a north-facing toilet orientation the first choice. Toilets aligned east to west are not recommended. Toilet fixtures and toilet rooms should not fall on the centerlines or corner-to-corner diagonals lines of the VPM.

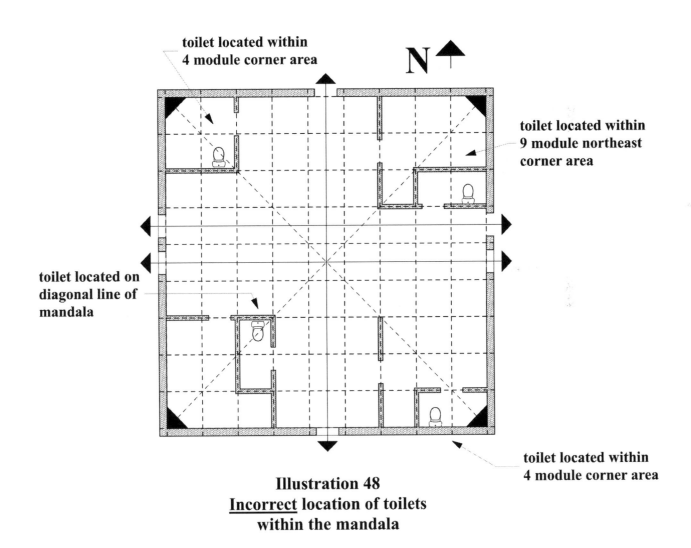

Illustration 48
Incorrect location of toilets
within the mandala

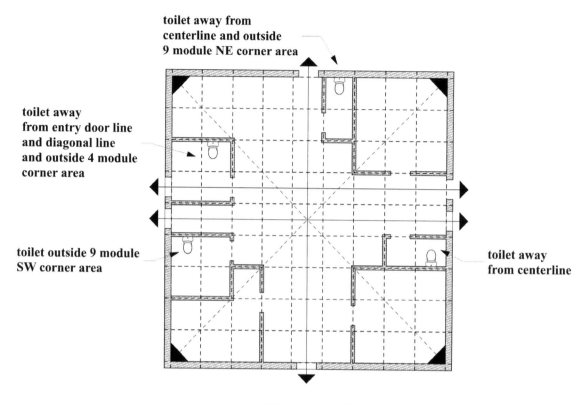

toilet away from centerline and outside 9 module NE corner area

toilet away from entry door line and diagonal line and outside 4 module corner area

toilet outside 9 module SW corner area

toilet away from centerline

Illustration 49
Example of a satisfactory location of toilets within the mandala

Bathrooms generally have a toilet, bathing area (shower, tub), and counter sink. The toilet location is the primary concern for location. Sink and bathing area locations and orientations are flexible. However, it's best not to locate a sink, shower, or tub on a centerline or diagonal line of the mandala. It's possible to have the bathing part of the bathroom within the mandala and the toilet area outside the mandala. This would be a good solution for keeping the extra square footage of an extension reduced. See

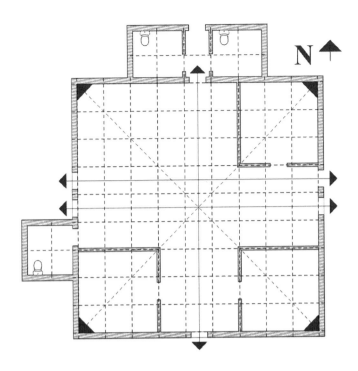

Illustration 50
Example of good locations for toilets
within extensions of the mandala

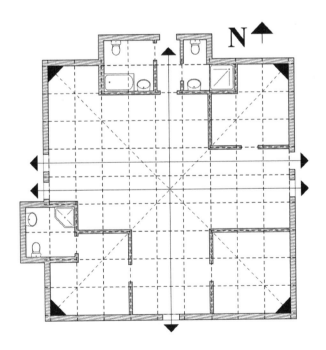

Illustration 51
Example of good locations for toilets
within partial extensions of the
mandala

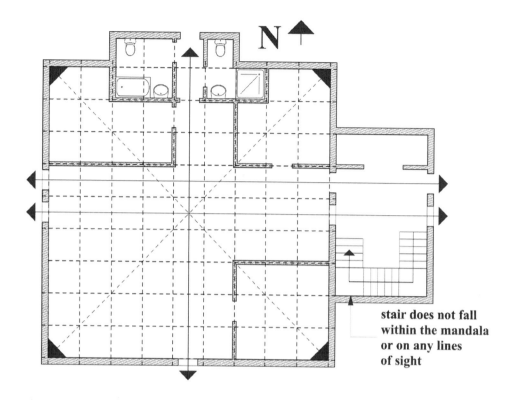

Illustration 52
Example of good location for
a stair outside the VPM

Stairs

Stairs are considered a disruptive element within the mandala of a Vastu structure. For this reason we must be careful to follow the simple rules of the science regarding the construction of stairs:

Rule 1: The ideal location of a stair is outside the Vastu Purusha Mandala in an extension to the mandala.

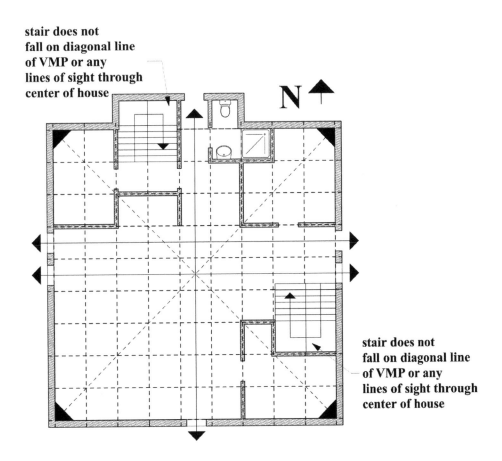

stair does not
fall on diagonal line
of VMP or any
lines of sight through
center of house

N

stair does not
fall on diagonal line
of VMP or any
lines of sight through
center of house

Illustration 53
Example of a good location for
a stair inside the VPM

Rule 2: If a stair is inside the mandala,

a) It should *not* be located on the diagonal lines that run through the mandala from southeast to northwest and southwest to northeast. These lines are powerful energy lines and should not be interrupted by a stair structure.

b) It should *not* be located on the centerlines of the mandala from east to west and north to south.

c) It should *not* be located on the line of sight from the main entry door to the opposite side of the structure.

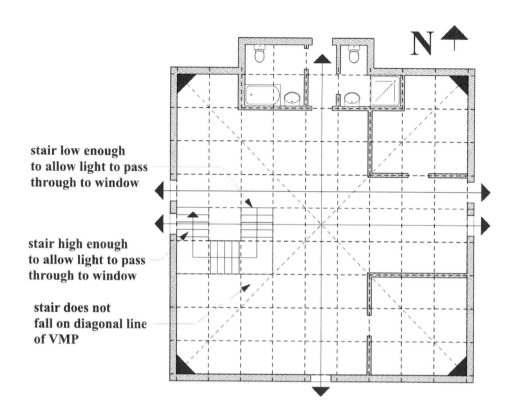

stair low enough
to allow light to pass
through to window

stair high enough
to allow light to pass
through to window

stair does not
fall on diagonal line
of VMP

Illustration 54
Example of acceptable location for
a stair when it lands on a centerline
of the VPM

However, if carefully designed by a Vastu professional, it is possible to place a stair on the centerlines in such a way that the lines of site through the structure are clear and open. The stair can be laid out so there are windows or doors under and above the stair structure, thus honoring the line of sight. This solution should only be used under the supervision of an experience Vastu architect.

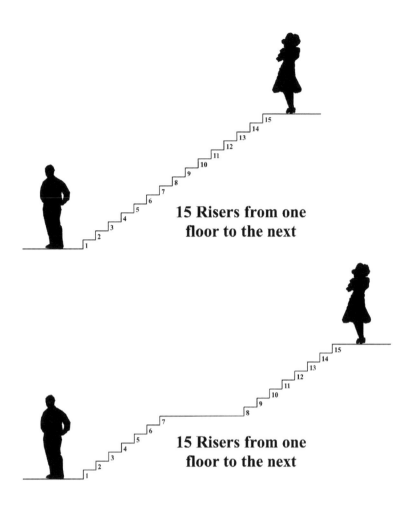

15 Risers from one floor to the next

15 Risers from one floor to the next

Illustration 55
Example of stair riser layout

Rule 3: In the stair construction, the number of risers should always be odd. Stairs have risers and treads. The riser is the vertical part of the stair. The tread is the horizontal part of the stair. As you ascend the stair, the number of "step-ups" should always be odd. Simply count the number of times you have to step up to reach the next floor and that is the number of risers in the stair. If the stair has landings, the landing is counted as one large tread.

Doing the math:

To design a stair in terms of dealing with treads and risers, simply take the distance from the top of the finished surface of one floor to the top of the finished surface of the next, and divide by an odd number while considering your target riser height.

Example: Floor to floor is 12'. Our target riser height is 7¼", so 12' ÷ 7¼" = 19.86. If we then divide 12' by 19 we get a riser height of about 7 9/16". This would be a suitable riser height, so the stair would have 19 risers.

Rule 4: The plan shape of the stair can be straight in any direction. This means you can begin ascending the stair facing any direction.

Rule 5: If the stair turns as it ascends, it should turn clockwise.

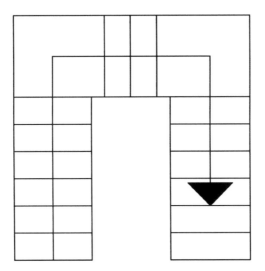

Illustration 56
17 risers
ascending clockwise

Ideally stairs are orthogonal in plan geometry. That is, if they turn they turn ninety degrees. Stairs can be L-shaped or U-shaped. Circular or semi-circular stairs are not compliant in Vastu structures. Stairs with round or elliptical plan geometries can be used if the client insists, but they are not ideal. If they are used, they would be best placed outside the mandala.

Rule 6: The stair plan should fall on the gridlines of the mandala if possible.

Zones of flexibility

The foundation of a Vastu structure is the Vastu Purusha Mandala (VPM). Room function locations are determined by the VPM, guided by the elemental influence in each of the four corners: Fire: southeast, Earth: southwest, Air: northwest, and Water: northeast. As stated, certain room functions are required due to elemental influences: the kitchen should be located in the southeast, the master bedroom should be in the southwest or south, the Puja room should be in the northeast, and Brahmastan is always located in the center. However, other areas in the mandala allow for flexibility of function. West, northwest, north, east, and south can be used for a number of occupancy functions. Note: In general the east area of the Mandala is good for health.

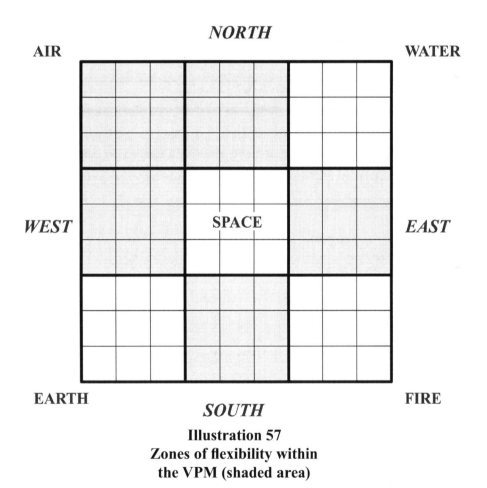

Illustration 57
Zones of flexibility within
the VPM (shaded area)

Bed location

As stated above the simple rule with beds is that when one is sleeping, the top of the head should be to the east or the south; both are equally acceptable. This rule applies to any sleeping location in the house. Individual astrology is not considered. This rule applies to all.

Mechanical rooms

Mechanical rooms include functions such as heating, cooling, electrical control, water heating, and laundering. The best area for heating, cooling, electrical control, and water heating is in the southeast area of the VPM or outside the mandala in extensions to the south-southeast or east-southeast. A secondary location for heating, cooling, electrical control, and water heating can be in the northwest area of the VPM or in extensions to the west-northwest or north-northwest. Laundries can be placed in locations following the rules for mechanical rooms or bathing rooms.

Location of service structures

In Dr. V. Ganapati Sthapati's excellent book, *The Building Architecture of Sthapatya Veda*, he refers to a prescription in the Mayamata that places a "vehicle" shed to the left side of the entrance of a structure of any orientation. In practice I have come to the opinion that service structures, such as a vehicle garage or barn or garden shed, can be placed in areas adjacent to the main structure such that they do not block the lines of light of the Vastu Purusha Mandala of the structure: 1) the thread of light in relationship to the front door, 2) the Brahma Sutra line and 3) the Soma Sutra line.

Along with the rule mentioned above, the basic rules I have used, based on inquiry, observation and practice are as follows:

1) Ideal placement of garage is detached from the main structure.

2) If garage is attached, separate by an intermediate hall.

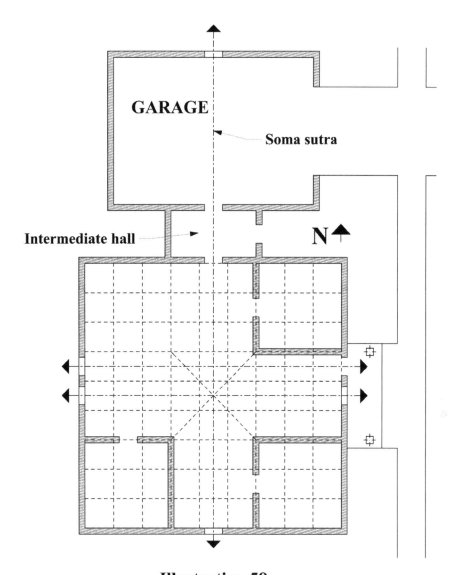

Illustration 58
Example of an attached Garage
with an intermediate hallway
leading to the perimeter of the Vastu
Purusha Mandala

3) If garage falls on a light line as mentioned above, extend the line of light through the garage also.

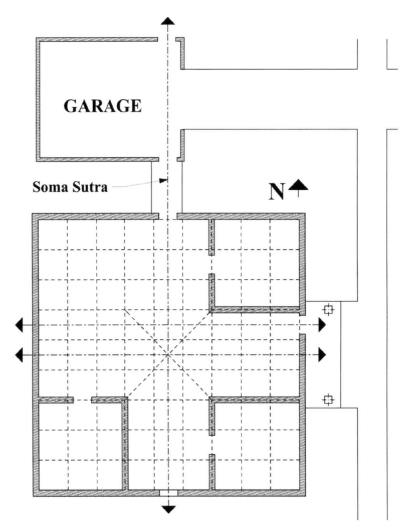

Illustration 59
Example of Soma sutra
extended through garage area

Also Sthapati's book mentions that the Mayamata and Manasara recommend the following locations for animal sheds:

Cow shed: southeast

Goat shed: southwest

Buffalo shed: northwest

Horse and elephant shed: northeast

Location of Wells

Water well location is very important. Well location shall be to the northeast of the structure. Distance is not important. Wells should not fall on the extended light lines of the house (thread of light from the front door, Brahma Sutra, and Soma Sutra). See illustrations below:

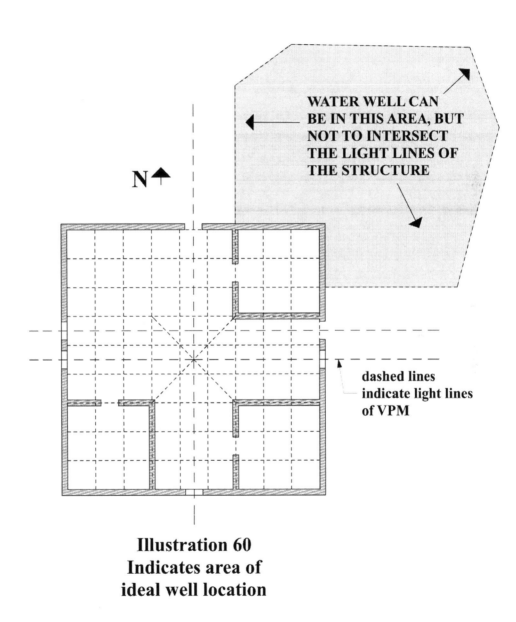

WATER WELL CAN BE IN THIS AREA, BUT NOT TO INTERSECT THE LIGHT LINES OF THE STRUCTURE

N

dashed lines indicate light lines of VPM

**Illustration 60
Indicates area of
ideal well location**

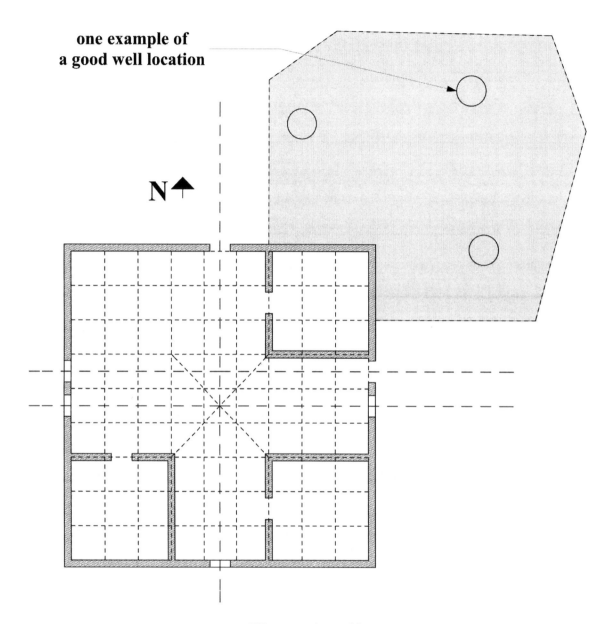

**one example of
a good well location**

N↑

**Illustration 61
Indicates some possible
well placements**

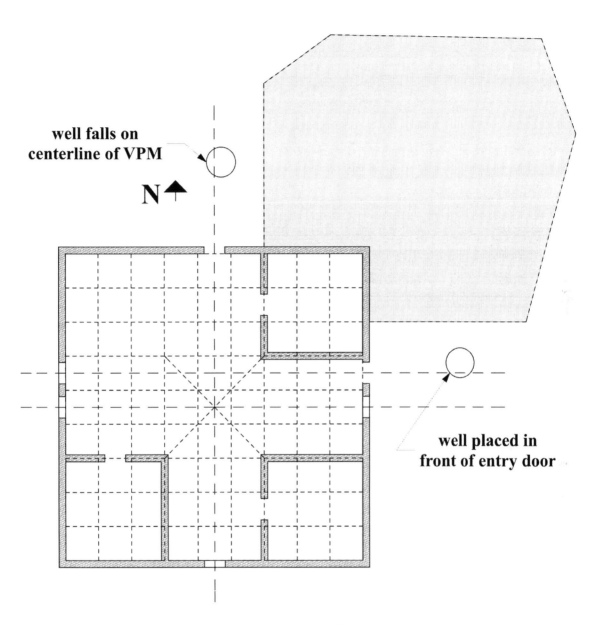

**well falls on
centerline of VPM**

N

**well placed in
front of entry door**

**Illustration 62
Examples of <u>incorrect</u>
well placement in
northeast quadrant**

Entry and exit locations for utilities

The Vastu structure is spatial form with the elemental energies of Earth, Air, Fire, and Water, and space fully enlivened in a specific spatial order. Because of this it is best to insert outside forms of energy, such as water, electricity and gas, at locations that are most compatible with these element zones. Also, exiting energy, specifically waste water, has designated routes.

Electricity and gas have fire energy; therefore, the ideal location for these services to enter into the structure is the Fire element area: the southeast corner of the Vastu Purusha Mandala. The water pipe should first enter the building in the northeast corner of the mandala. These services can come in from either side of their respective corners. Alternate entry locations for electricity, gas, and water are allowed. Electricity and gas could enter at the northwest corner area and water could enter at the southwest corner area, but these locations are only to be used when circumstances disallow the recommended locations.

Waste water pipes exiting the house should cross the Vastu Purusha Mandala boundary away from corners and light lines. If there is a waste water collection tank and drainage field, they should be outside the Vastu fence. The tank should not fall on the extended energy lines of the mandala, as illustrated below. Waste water tanks should be kept out of the east and northeast areas.

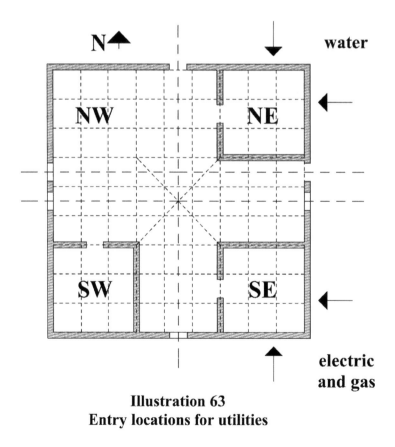

Illustration 63
Entry locations for utilities

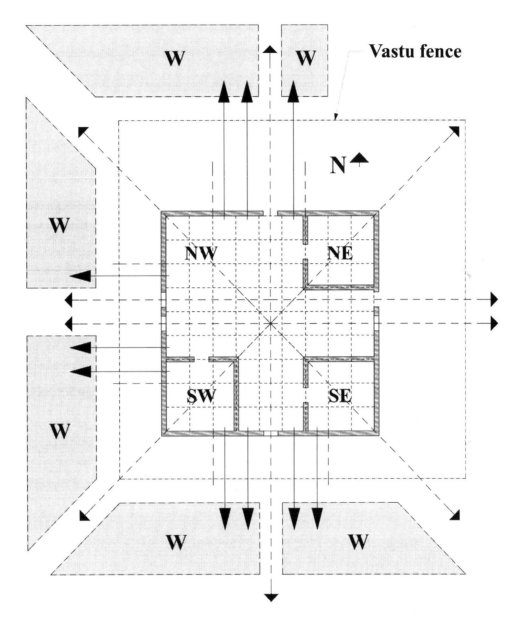

Illustration 64
Shaded areas (W) indicate where
wastewater collection tank could be placed

■ What you learned in this chapter:

1) The Vastu structure is based on an underlying geometry called a Vastu Purusha Mandala (VPM).

2) The VPM is a geometric paradigm that gives the Vastu structures its ability to resonate with earth and cosmic energy matrices.

3) The VPM uses specific units of measure unique to Vastu science that create a three-dimensional space that is highly energized.

4) The main entry of the Vastu structure is specifically placed for all benefits and should be used most often to enter the building.

5) The walls of the Vastu structure have a direct relationship to the VPM.

6) A Vastu structure has prescribed proportions and patterns.

7) The center area of a Vastu structure is called the Brahmastan: the sacred center space of the building.

8) Each Vastu structure is protected within a Vastu yard that is created by surrounding the building with a wall that has a prescribed location and dimensions, depending on the VPM for that structure.

9) Vastu structures require extra care during construction to insure that all elements of the building are in correct position.

10) Within the VPM of the structure, specific activities have prescribed locations. These prescriptions should be followed to achieve beneficial results.

11) Some functions within modern structures have a polluting influence (such as toilets and stairs), and, therefore, need to be specifically located to mitigate negative effects.

4. Creating a Three-Dimensional Vastu-Compliant Structure

The Vastu Purusha Mandala is a geometry that is not only applied to the floor plan of the structure. The module of the VPM is employed in the vertical as well as horizontal design of the structure. The Vastu building is a living object, a body with life. As a living form, the structure requires a beauty that comes from measures and proportions applied from the geometry of the two dimensional VPM.

In temple design a protocol is in place to create a building that embodies a strict order of anthropomorphic parts. These parts are Upapeetam (base/foot), Adisthaanam (base/leg), Paadam (walls and pillars/trunk and hands), Prastram (roof/shoulders), Greevam (transition to cupola/neck), Shikaram (cupola/head), Stupi (kalash/hair tuft).

In a secular structure, this list is simplified to base (plinth), wall, roof and kalash. The Vastu architect's assignment is to incorporate the module of the VPM during the composition of the building elevations.

Note: The base of the building, the plinth, can be a decorative element incorporated into the wall of the structure in relationship to the Vastu module, or it can be an actual structural base, for example an exposed foundation wall.

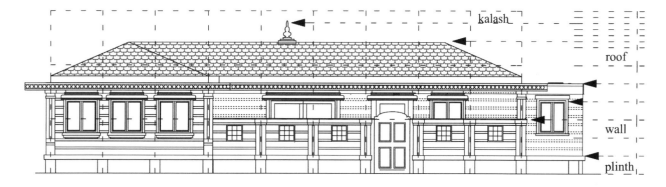

Illustration 65
Laangala Griham East Elevation Study with module overlay

The interior space of the building also incorporates the module.

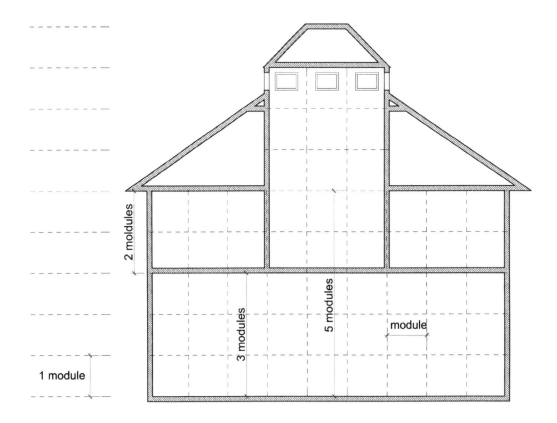

Illustration 66
Example of modulated space
within the Vastu structure

By combining the VPM in the floor plan and the VPM module in the elevations and interior space of the building, the architect creates a space that is vibrant with Vastu energy.

Important Note: If the Vastu Purusha Mandala of the structure is not employing a 1:1 proportion, the module used for elevation composition and vertical interior space is the unit *width* value.

For example,

Mandala perimeter Ayadi value = 55

Vastu unit value = 2'9"

Perimeter value of the Vastu Purusha = 151'3"

Proportion of mandala = 1:2

Therefore: width = 25'2 ½"; width module = 25'2 ½" ÷ 9 = 2'9⅝"

length = 50'5"; length module = 50'5" ÷ 9 = 5'7 7/32"

The unit used for elevation composition and interior vertical space is the width value of 2'9⅝".

Roof Slope:

Illustrated below are the accepted roof slopes for a Vastu structure 5:12. 9:12 and 16:12. Another roof slope, also accepted, is 12:12 slope. Use these roof slope values whenever possible. If using a non-compliant roof slope, keep it in compliance with the vertical module values. For example, if the structure has a flat roof, compose the elevation such that the top of roof is relating to the ruling module of the Vastu Purusha Mandala.

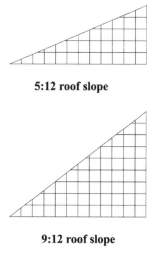

5:12 roof slope

9:12 roof slope

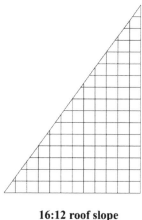

16:12 roof slope

Illustration 67
Recommended roof slopes

The overall massing of a Vastu structure is usually fairly symmetric as a three-dimensional object. However, sometimes an experienced Vastu architect can create a pleasing composition that is not symmetric. If the structure is asymmetric, the highest parts (or masses) of the structure should be in the south, southwest or west. This means the building would be taller in those areas and lower to the north, northeast or east. However, it is *not* correct, as some propose, to make the walls on the west and south more thick and heavy. Please do not imbalance the structure by doing this.

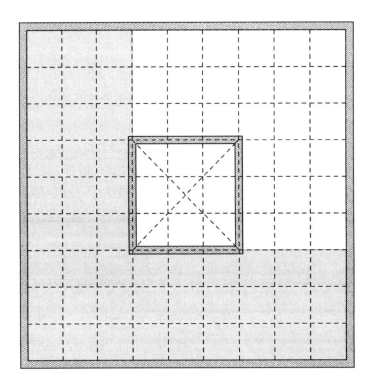

Illustration 68
Indicates areas (shaded) where taller
parts of the structure are allowed in an
asymmetrical composition

■ **What you learned in this chapter:**

A) A Vastu structure is a three-dimensional expression of sacred geometry, employing specific building shapes, proportions, and composition to create a living, energizing space to occupy.

5. Materials

The ideal materials for a Vastu structure are—as my teacher put it—"Mother's" materials. By this he meant materials from Mother Earth: wood, stone, and earth. These materials allow the structure to generate the most healing resonance with the land on which it is placed and the human that resides within it.

Examples of natural materials:

1) Adobe

2) Straw bale and earthen plaster

3) Compressed straw clay mixture

4) Rammed earth

5) Wood: timber frame and stick frame (with a natural insulation), log

6) Stone (Solid stone structures are not recommended for houses.)

However, in some modern structures, it can be problematic to build simply with wood, stone, and earth. Around the world the standard construction materials vary, depending on the local resources and building practices.

In the U.S. the standard is to build with a wood frame (called "stick frame" construction) and cover the hollow framed walls with an interior layer of gypsum board and various exterior materials. In my opinion these structures are fairly benign in terms of Vastu, especially if the designer specifies "green" products as much as possible. Insulation can be cotton batts. Interior surface finishes can be non-toxic. Wood, tile, and stone can be used to create an environment that has a clean earth influence. Also, the framed wall construction method gives a fairly good opportunity to achieve accurate dimensions. In the structure of the wood-framed building, the designer should try to avoid using steel as much as possible, especially large steel bodies like heavy I-beams and posts. In the concrete foundation, if possible the reinforcement should be fiberglass rod instead of steel. The reason for this is that metals may attract disruptive energies. (However, I have been involved in many Vastu structures that used standard steel rebar for structural reinforcement, and these buildings seem to be fine in terms of an energetic signature.)

In Asia the new standard is to build a concrete superstructure and infill with masonry units (usually a low-density fired brick). Steel is heavily used in such structures for reinforcing the concrete columns, beams, and floor slabs. This is not ideal for a Vastu structure. However, I did design and build a large factory complex in Asia that used this typical construction method, and the factory seemed to have a very prosperous effect for the owners. Also, it is difficult to achieve the high degree of accuracy required in a Vastu project with a concrete superstructure. It can be done, but it is a challenge.

Mechanical and electrical systems are also somewhat disruptive for energy. However, these systems are unavoidable in a modern building. The most important factor regarding these systems is to keep them out of the Brahmastan of the building. Air vents, plumbing pipes, electrical cables, in-floor heating pipes, and such should not run through the area of the Brahmastan. However, these mechanical items can be placed in walls around the perimeter of the Brahmastan. A limited amount of lighting and/or a fan could be placed in the ceiling of the Brahmastan.

Ideally a Vastu building would be built on the ground with earth, stone, and wood and have no mechanical systems. This would create a supremely pure and silence soaked environment. In such a structure, human beings could live humbly in the spaces around the perimeter of the Brahmastan, thriving in the blessed radiance of cosmic energy.

■ **What you learned in this chapter:**

1) Natural earth-based materials are best to use for Vastu structures.

2) Modern building systems and materials can be used in Vastu structures if used judiciously.

6. Protocols for Building and Living in a Vastu Structure

The following list can be reprinted and given as the basic protocols to be followed when building a Vastu structure:

1) The center space, called the Brahmastan, is the heart of the house. It is a powerful energy space. It is best if it is left open and free. Do not clutter it with excess furniture. Furniture can be in the Brahmastan if placed in a way that does not interfere with the exact center of the space. Anything put in the Brahmastan will influence the energy of the house. No water or fire elements should be placed there. No plants. Also, absolutely no mechanical, plumbing, or electrical systems should run through the Brahmastan.

2) The southwest area of the house is for the master of the house (the wife and husband) to rest and recuperate. Find some time to rest (or sleep) in this area each day, if possible.

3) The southeast area of the house is where cooking takes place. Each day the lady of the house should stand at the cook stove facing east and prepare something, even if it is only tea.

4) The dimensions of the house, as dictated by the Vastu Purusha Mandala and provided by the Vastu architect, are very important. When followed precisely they allow the house to have a geometry and proportion that is resonant with healing and nurturing energies. The project architect *must* make it clear to all contractors from the beginning that this Vastu project is extremely demanding with regard to the dimensions. All dimensions are to be followed exactly, and the project architect is responsible to verify the dimensions and call for corrections if they are needed.

5) A surveyor shall be required to site the house with the proper orientation. A west- or east-facing house shall be oriented such that it is rotated *counterclockwise* one and a half degrees from *true* perfect orientation to the cardinal points of the compass. A north- or south-facing house shall be oriented such that it is rotated *clockwise* one and a half degrees from *true* perfect orientation to the cardinal points of the compass. *True* north is *not* magnetic north. The surveyor must be relating to *true* north.

The surveyor must give the layout lines for correct orientation before the foundation is excavated, and these lines shall maintain their integrity for verifying the orientation throughout the project. The project architect or project contractor shall be responsible for the correctness of building orientation and verify it with a surveyor at the following milestones of construction:

A) Before excavation,

B) After foundation forming and before the concrete is placed in the forms,

C) After the concrete forms are stripped and before the construction of the walls begins.

Dimensions shall be checked:

A) After the foundation is formed and before it is poured,

B) After the foundation is poured and stripped. At this time, it can be determined if any corrections are needed in the framing layout to get back to correct dimensions,

C) During the wall construction, the contractor and architect shall check dimensions and make sure the builders are honoring the layout.

The object of these protocols is to have the goal of honoring the dimensions at all times to the 1/16" (1.5mm). The tape measure has that dimension and a pencil mark can be made to the 1/16" mark as easy as the 1" mark. It is understood that with all types of construction, the dimensions will be slightly off perfection and may even change during construction due to weather and material properties. If the builder honors the dimension every time he (she) measures a layout, then the discrepancies will be kept to a minimum. Any discrepancies shall be reported to the client and the Vastu designer as soon as they have been identified.

6) Entry doors: whenever possible the main entry door should be used. This door is located in a position that brings specific beneficial effects. Use this door as much as possible when leaving the house in the morning and coming home at night. Also, use this door for all the special occasions and events in life.

6) "Milestone" ceremonies shall be performed at the following times during the project: 1) groundbreaking, 2) foundation stone deposit, and 3) moving-in day. The time and date of these ceremonies need to be given by an expert Vastu consultant or Vedic astrological consultant. There are eight Puja dates a year specifically appropriate for Vastu milestone ceremonies. Your Vastu consultant can give the dates.

These traditional formal ceremonies—groundbreaking, laying the foundation stone, and moving-in—are conducted at these "auspicious times;" but they are in Tamil or Sanskrit, so they are not available to us except if we engage a Vastu pundit. If you choose to contact a priest at your local Hindu temple, you may have the priest conduct the appropriate ceremonies for each of these occasions. The recommended ceremonies are 1) Ganapati Puja, 2) Vastu Puja, and 3) Satyanarayana Puja.

My teacher, Ganapati Sthapati, has always encouraged me to conduct my own ceremony, telling me to use my own inner knowledge of what to do. If we come from the heart, with a good intention for the living structure and also with respect for Mother Earth upon which the home sits rooted in Earth energies, the building will be blessed. Just a simple ceremony should be conducted at the auspicious time. Work beginning at this time will be completed without any impediment, and the finished building will yield prosperity, wealth, and longevity.

The main purpose of these ceremonies is to achieve a deep sense of harmony with the Earth energy, Mother Earth, the spirit of the house, and the blessing energies of the masters of the knowledge of Vastu science. These ceremonies arouse cosmic forces, directing them in a positive way for the project.

At an auspicious time, a foundation deposit can be placed for the house. This deposit consists of precious gems and metals. It should be placed so that it will not be disturbed during construction. The gems placed in the foundation deposit are to be arranged in a simple pattern as illustrated below. Also, if you so desire, a small deposit of gold, silver, and copper may be added to the foundation deposit. When fixing the orientation of the gem plate, make sure the pearl is *oriented to the north*. The gems can be placed in a small protecting box of some sort.

Note: If the owner of the structure desires to add more gifts, an additional gem plate can be placed under the hinge side of the base of the frame of the main entry door and under the base of the Kalash at the top of the structure..

NORTH

hesonite	pearl	spartika
emerald	ruby	diamond
topaz	blue sapphire	coral

SOUTH

Illustration 69
Gem plate layout for foundation
deposit in the Vastu structure

Note: Hessonite or cinnamon stone is a variety of grossular, a calcium aluminum mineral of the garnet group. Spartika is clear quartz crystal.

These stones differ slightly from the stones traditionally used to represent the nine planets. These stones that are used for Vastu Puja do not refer to the planets. They are "seeds of the earth" that are placed to add sweetness to the Vastu structure. Dr. V. Ganapati Sthapati says that you can think about these stones as a nice addition to any Vastu structure. Sthapati gave this analogy about the gems: If you have a cup of coffee, it is, of itself, fully coffee. If you add a little sugar to it, you sweeten it. If you add too much sugar, you spoil it. In that same way, a few small gems are not required for a Vastu structure, but they add a nice flavor (and therefore they are recommended). I have personally arrived at the opinion that a Vastu structure doesn't *need* anything added to make it powerful or effective. It is effective and powerful of itself. Adding the gems and metals is a performance that embellishes the inherent sweetness of the structure. It is recommended.

A further refinement of the foundation deposit can include a gem plate overlaid by protecting tiles inscribed with Tamil vowels "a," "e," "o," "u," and "i." (For details on this, contact the author.)

The installation method is as follows:
Place the gems in the depression made to receive them, using the correct orientation. Then place sand over the gem deposit. Create a level area and place the tiles in the configuration shown in the photograph. Then place more sand and then earth or cement over the whole area to protect the deposit. Make sure that this area is not disturbed during the rest of construction.

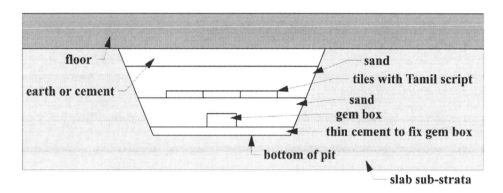

Illustration 70
Diagram of the foundation deposit
construction

To begin preparing for the groundbreaking ceremony, stake the perimeter of the building. At least locate the area of the northeast corner of the Vastu Purusha Mandala of the building. At the proper time, as instructed by your consultant, you can begin the ceremony you have created to honor the event.

If you are creating your own ceremony, if you so desire, you can use this prayer:

Protector of the dwelling, recognize us: Be an excellent abode, the non-inflictor of disease.
Whatever we ask of thee, be pleased to grant. Bestow happiness on our bipeds and quadrupeds.
Protector of the dwelling, be the preserver and augmenter of our wealth.
Possessed of cattle and horses, Indra, may we, through thy friendship, be exempt from decay: like
a father to his sons, be favorable to us. Protector of the dwelling, may we be possessed of a comfort-
able, delightful, opulent abode bestowed by thee.
Protect our wealth, whether in possession or expectation, and ever cherish us with blessings.
Protector of the dwelling, remover of disease, assuming all kinds of forms, be to us a friend:
the grantor of happiness!

Place the foundation deposit at this time. The exact location of that pit is illustrated below.

In a typical Western house, it's possible to make a depression in the concrete slab of the house during construction. At the proper time, we come back and place the foundation deposit.

■ What you learned in this chapter:

1) The Brahmastan is the sacred center of the house. It should be honored as such and kept free of all mechanical and electrical systems.

2) A basic paradigm of living in a Vastu house is to use the southwest area of the VPM for the master bedroom and the southeast area of the VPM for the kitchen.

3) The Vastu-dictated dimensions are very important and must be honored at all times.

4) Construction protocols should be followed to insure the integrity of the Vastu structure.

5) The regular use of the prescribed main entry door is recommended.

6) Milestone ceremonies are recommended in the creation of a Vastu building.

N↑

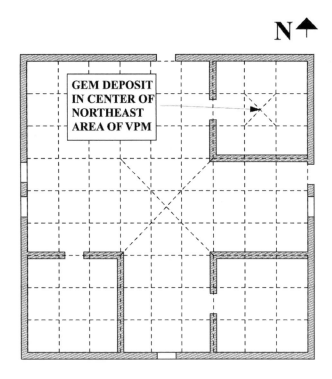

GEM DEPOSIT IN CENTER OF NORTHEAST AREA OF VPM

Illustration 71
Location of the gem deposit within
the mandala in the northeast area

7. Ayadi Calculations

Ayadi calculations are the ancient mathematic formulas used by the expert Vastu scientists/artists to assign the vibration or frequency of a physical form and to create an energizing and healing resonance within the structure. If Ayadi calculations are not involved, it is not likely that the form will vibrate in resonance with Earth and cosmic energy matrices.

Ayadi applications are rooted in a deep cognition and understanding of how the energetic, but gross, material universe comes into existence, springing from primal unmanifest Source Energy. The expression of Ayadi is found in prescribed mathematical units used to create fully vibrant living organic forms: music, poetry, bodily postures and movements (sacred dance), sculpture, and architecture.

Such resonance with Source gives life.

From Dr. V. Ganapati Sthapati's foundational treatise on sacred architecture, *The Building Architecture of Sthapatya Veda*, I take a quote by Mayan:

Architecture is the supreme achievement of mathematics and this mathematics is rooted in the computation of Absolute Time. This means Absolute Time created life, and Vastu Shastras enshrine the technological interpretation and the methodology for creating living organisms for human welfare and well-being.

A simple way to understand how the mathematics of a physical structure can achieve resonance is the example of the technology of a tuning fork. This instrument is designed to predictably and precisely reproduce a given frequency of vibration called a musical note. Each note is founded in a specific frequency value that is the result of the geometry of a physical structure that is energized and therefore vibrating. What distinguishes one tuning fork from another is mathematics of form: ratio of length to breadth to width.

For example, a middle C tuning fork vibrates at a frequency of 262 Hz. (From Wikipedia; I add the italicized text): "The hertz (symbol: Hz) is a measure of frequency per unit of time, or the number of cycles per second…Hertz can be used to measure any periodic event; the most common uses for hertz are to describe radio and audio frequencies, more or less sinusoidal contexts in which case a frequency of one Hz is equal to one cycle per second…*Acoustic resonance* is the tendency of an acoustic system *(or structure)* to absorb more energy when the frequency of its oscillations matches the system's *(or structure's)* natural frequency of vibration *(its resonance frequency)* than it does at other frequencies."

"If we were to seek acoustic resonance with a physical structure *(a tuning fork)* that vibrates at 262Hz, we would need to create a structure that has the same physical geometric configuration or one that has a configuration that has a specific and exact relationship to that geometry. The relationship that creates the most resonance is one in which the geometry of one structure to the other has a ratio of 1:1 (exactly the same) or 1:2 or 1:4, etc. All C's are successively one half or double the frequency of middle C. The C above middle C, one octave above, vibrates at 524Hz."

When we energize a middle C tuning fork by striking it, it emits a wave energy that can be absorbed by other physical structures. If that structure is another C tuning fork of any frequency, it will be able to receive or absorb a good deal of the energy due its geometric resonance, and therefore it will vibrate. However, if the energy wave from middle C tuning fork strikes an F tuning fork above or below middle C, that fork will be less able to energize or vibrate. The F tuning fork will be silent, not energized. In fact, a middle C tuning fork structure will identify its resonant frequency from a complex exposure of energy frequencies, filtering out all frequencies except its resonant ones. This is a key goal of a Vastu structure: filtering dissonant energy and absorbing sonant energy.

Vastu structures are designed using precise mathematical units and geometries to resonate with Source Energy systems, and due to this resonance, they vibrate with life energy. Energy systems we witness in nature, such as a star or a solar system or an Earth or a human or a tree or an ant, have life energy due to geometric resonance with universal and subtle energy systems. Ayadi calculations are the formulas the Vastu technician uses to give the created object perfect resonance with subtle universal cosmic energy.

Ayadi calculations in practical application

Vastu science regards life as universal. All life is connected. The universe is a complete living organism communicating with and influencing every corner of itself. Living organisms are usually fairly unique in physical composition, characteristics, and tendencies. Vastu science attributes these differences to the influence of planetary and stellar energy emanations. A human organism—also a physical structure called a building—is influenced during its conception and birth by cosmic influences.

When a new Vastu creation is conceived, the artist/scientist considers carefully the existing environmental composition, characteristics, and tendencies of all significant organisms that will come into relationship with that creation and precisely chooses a resonant and harmonious combination.

The main factor in determining resonance is the "birth star" of the organism. The birth star is the *lunar* Nakshatra as determined by an expert Jyotish consultant (see chart below). Each birth star has a unique influence, imparting a particular vibration or frequency to the organism. Human beings have a birth star or frequency set at birth, and the Vastu expert chooses a frequency for the Vastu structure that is compatible and life enhancing for all who occupy the space. In Vastu science this is called Ayadi Gananam.

NAKSHATRA CHART		
Column 1	Column 2	Column 3
1-Ashwini (Ketu)	10-Makha (Ketu)	19-Moola (Ketu)
2-Bharai (Venus)	11-Poorva Phal (Venus)	20-Poorva Ashada (Venus)
3-Krithika (Sun)	12-Uttara Phal (Sun)	21-Uttara Ashada (Sun)
4-Rohini (Moon)	13-Hasta (Moon)	22-Sravana (Thiru) (Moon)
5-Mrigishira (Mars)	14-Chitra (Mars)	23-Dhanishta (Mars)
6-Aridra (Tiru) (Rahu)	15-Swati (Rahu)	24-Satabhish (Rahu)
7-Purnavasu (Jupiter)	16-Vishaka (Jupiter)	25-Poorva Bhad (Jupiter)
8-Pushyami (Saturn)	17-Anuradha (Saturn)	26-Uttara Bhad (Saturn)
9-Aslesha (Mercury)	18-Jeyshta (Kettai) (Mercury)	27-Revati (Mercury)

In a Vastu building, the frequency is set by the measure of the perimeter of the Vastu Purusha Mandala that is generated for the building. The Vastu architect arrives at the building frequency by applying various Ayadi formulas that define particular important aspects or characteristics of that frequency. To begin with the designer can impose six formulas and this set is called Sadayadi. Also there is the option of applying ten formulas (Dasayadi) or sixteen formulas (Shodasayadi or Poornayadi). Sayayadi (six formulas) is accepted for secular buildings. However, for sacred buildings Shodasayadi (sixteen formulas) should be used.

The scientific formulas are applied to a numerical value chosen by the Vastu architect, and predictable results are defined by the solution to each formula. The point is to achieve a building that has a mathematical value (frequency) that gives positive solutions to at least the six formulas known as

Sayayadi. Creating a building that gives positive solutions to the prescribed ten or sixteen formulas is desirable but not necessary for secular buildings.

The numerical value used is not a common unit of measure like British imperial units or metric units. The numerical value used for the Vastu Purusha Mandala (VPM) is the value of the energy wave or frequency of the mandala, and specific numbers are used in Vastu science for creating objects that vibrate with good effects. For example, 107 is a numerical value used for a VPM. This value can be applied to standard units of measure utilized by Vastu designers.

Some Vastu space unit measures:

kishku hastam = 2'9"

½ kishku hastam (vitasti) = 1'4½"

¼ kishku hastam (taalam) = 8¼"

angula = 1⅜"

8 kishku hastam = 1 dandam = 22'0"

8 dandam = 1 rajju = 176'0"

The designer can apply the frequency value of 107 to any of these units. If it is applied to 2'9", the perimeter value of the VPM would be 107 x 2'9" = 294'3." If the mandala side proportions are 1:1 (a square), then the side value of the mandala would be 73'6¾". This would create a building with 73'6¾" on each side of the main exterior wall dimensions. The designer could also use 107 x 1'4½"(vitasti), and the perimeter value would be 147'1½" with sides of 36'9⅜".

For a town plan, the designer might apply 107 x 176'(1 raju) = 18,832' perimeter value. This would give a square town plan with boundary wall lines of 4,708'.

In each case the perimeter value sets the energy wave or frequency of the structure. The structure will vibrate with a specific energy that will create a positive influence for the inhabitants.

Perimeter value of the mandala must always take the form of a square or rectangle with specific side length ratios. The accepted prime ratios are 1:1, 1:1.25, 1:1.5, 1:1.75, and 1:2. Other ratios that are accepted by not often used (they can be considered secondary to the prime ratios) are 1:1 1/9, 1:1 2/9, 1:1/3, 1:1 4/9, 1:1 5/9, 1:1 2/3, 1:1 7/9, 1:1 8/9, and 1:3.

An example of how to align frequency of structure with frequency of occupants

Example factors:

- Residential structure for a large extended family (the Smith Family)

- Target size: 6,000 to 7,000 square feet (single floor structure)

- Facing of building: east

- Building owners: husband and wife

- Other occupants: two daughters, one son, two elderly parents

Having discussed the specific program in terms of size, orientation, room requirement, etc., the Vastu designer takes the following steps to arrive at a good VPM for the structure and the family.

Step one:

Determine the birth star (_lunar_ Nakshatra) of all occupants:

(We determine the birth star by contacting an expert Jyotish consultant.)

The lunar nakshatras we will use in the example shall be:

Mother: Poorva Phalguni

Father: Krithika

Daughter One: Uttara Ashada

Daughter Two: Satabhish

Son: Chitra

Grandfather: Krithika

Grandmother: Purnavasu

Step two:

Choosing a target size for the VPM based on the desired square footage of the building: The target size of the structure is 6,000 to 7,000 square feet, so the designer must choose a mandala that will have a square footage that falls near this target. (For this exercise we will assume we are choosing to use a square VPM.) We determine that a mandala that encompasses 6,000 square feet has sides of about 77'6." We choose a target mandala toward the lower value of square footage because we know we will want to build extensions on the building outside of the mandala for the services (toilets, etc.) that are best kept outside the VPM, so 77'6" gives us a target perimeter value of 310'0."

Step three:

Roughly translate the target perimeter (310'0") into Vastu units.

310'0" ÷ 2'9" = roughly 112 (hasta)

310'0" ÷ 1'4½" = roughly 225½ (vitasti)

310'0" ÷ 8¼" = roughly 450¼ (taalam)

310'0" ÷ 1⅜" = roughly 2,705 (angula)

Step four:

Application of Ayadi calculations to determine a positive value for the mandala:

The first priority is to find a VPM measured in hastas, then vitasti, then taalam. For this structure we will not consider the use of angulas in giving a unit value to the mandala. Because the angula is such a small unit, the margin of error grows large in a structure of this size.

Sadayadi set of Ayadi formulas

Formula one: Nakshatra = Ayadi number x 8/27

For demonstration we will work with two number values simultaneously:

A) 112

B) 107

112 x 8/27 = 896/27 = 33 5/27

107 x 8/27 = 856/27 = 31 19/27

The key number value is the remainder of the division, which is 5 (for 112) and 19 (for 107). This indicates that if we use a mandala of 112 hastas, the Nakshatra value will be 5. If we use a mandala value of 107 hastas, the Nakshatra value will be 19. This will be the frequency of the structure. (Note: in common practice, an even number of any Vastu unit is never used. For the purposes of illustration, we will work with 112.)

Now we can refer to the Nakshatra table (For convenience I have placed it in two locations in the text:

NAKSHATRA CHART		
Column 1	Column 2	Column 3
1-Ashwini (Ketu)	10-Makha (Ketu)	19-Moola (Ketu)
2-Bharai (Venus)	11-Poorva Phal (Venus)	20-Poorva Ashada (Venus)
3-Krithika (Sun)	12-Uttara Phal (Sun)	21-Uttara Ashada (Sun)
4-Rohini (Moon)	13-Hasta (Moon)	22-Sravana (Thiru) (Moon)
5-Mrigishira (Mars)	14-Chitra (Mars)	23-Dhanishta (Mars)
6-Aridra (Tiru) (Rahu)	15-Swati (Rahu)	24-Satabhish (Rahu)
7-Purnavasu (Jupiter)	16-Vishaka (Jupiter)	25-Poorva Bhad (Jupiter)
8-Pushyami (Saturn)	17-Anuradha (Saturn)	26-Uttara Bhad (Saturn)
9-Aslesha (Mercury)	18-Jeyshta (Kettai) (Mercury)	27-Revati (Mercury)

Referring to the table, the remainder value of 5 indicates that the Nakshatra of the 112 mandala will be Mrigishira, the remainder value of 19 indicates that the Nakshatra of the 107 mandala will be Moola.

At this point we have two possible frequency values for the structure: Mrigishira (5) and Moola (19).

Step five:
Investigate the relationship between the Nakshatra of the house and the Nakshatra of the occupants of the house.

The priority list for compatibility with the Nakshatra of the structure is as follows:

1) wife (mistress of the house)

2) husband (master of the house)

3) eldest child

4) next child, etc.

5) elders

The mistress of the house is taken as first priority because her health, welfare, and happiness will set the foundation for good in the entire household. However, the Vastu designer will try to work down the list of occupants for positive relationships for all.

Nakshatra compatibility is determined by relationship of the human frequency (Nakshatra) to building frequency. The Vastu designer refers to the Nakshatra table and counts the stars starting from that of the human. Once this count is made, the number achieved is applied to the Paryaya table.

Paryaya table

(Benefit or malady)

1. Janmam: rebirth (OK for Devas)

2. Sampath: wealth, prosperity

3. Vipath: accident

4. Kshemam: welfare

5. Pratyaram: neutral

6. Sadhakam: beneficial

7. Vadham: death

8. Maitram: friendship

9. Parama Maitram: supreme friendship

Referring again to our two examples:
Building Nakshatra = Example A: Mrigishira; Example B: Moola

Example A: For Mrigishira building Nakshatra, taking the wife's lunar Nakshatra: Poorva Phalguni (11):

We count the Nakshatras from Poorva Phalguni (11) to Mrigishira (5), including Poorva Phalguni. 1. Poorva Phalguni, 2. Uttara Phalguni, 3. Hasta, 4. Chitra, 5. Swati, 6. Vishaka, 7. Anuradha, 8. Jeyshta, 9. Moola, 1. Poorva Ashada, 2. Uttara Ashada,
3. Sravana, 4. Dhanishta, 5. Satabhish, 6. Poorva Bhadaras, 7. Uttara Bhadaras,
8. Revati, 9. Ashwini, 1. Bharai, 2. Krithika, 3. Rohini, 4. Mrigishira.

The relationship value, called paryaya, of wife's lunar Nashatra to building Nakshtra (determined by building perimeter value expressed in Vastu units) has the value of 4. Referring to the paryaya table, we see that the paryaya value of 4 gives the benefit of "welfare." This is acceptable. The Nakshatra of the structure will have the influence of welfare on the wife. In fact, paryaya values of 2,4,6,8, and 9 are always accepted. A paryaya value of 5 can be accepted under specific circumstances that will be illustrated below.

Example B: For Moola building Nakshatra, taking the wife's lunar Nakshatra: Poorva Phalguni (11): We count the Nakshatras from Poorva Phalguni (11) to Moola (19), including Poorva Phalguni. 1.Poorva Phalguni, 2. Uttara Phalguni, 3.Hasta, 4. Chitra.5 – Swati, 6. Vishaka, 7. Anuradha, 8. Jeyshta, 9. Moola. The relationship value, paryaya, of wife's lunar Nashatra to building Nakshtra (determined by building perimeter value expressed in Vastu units) has the value of 9. Referring to the paryaya table below, we see that the paryaya value of 9 gives the benefit of "supreme friendship." This is acceptable. The Nakshatra of the structure will have the influence of supreme friendship on the wife.

According to these investigations, we find that both options for Nakshatra of the house are good for the wife.

Continuing with our investigation, the husband is now considered:

Example A: Father's Nakshatra is Krithika. *Counting* from Krithika to Mrigishira:
1. Krithika, 2. Rohini, 3. Mrigishira.

The paryaya value of the husband's lunar Nashatra to building Nakshtra has the value of 3. Referring to the paryaya table below, we see that the paryaya value of 3 gives the malady of "accident." This is not acceptable. The Nakshatra of the structure will have a negative influence on the husband. At this point we *abandon* consideration of using Mrigishira for the Nakshatra of the structure and we investigate Moola.

Example B: Father's Nakshatra is Krithika. *Counting* from Krithika to Moola:
1. Krithika, 2. Rohini, 3. Mrigishira, 4.Aridra, 5. Purnavasu, 6. Pushyami,
7. Aslesha, 8. Makha, 9. Poorva Phalguni; (then we begin with one), 1. Uttara Phalguni, 2. Hasta,
3. Chitra, 4. Swati, 5.Vishaka, 6. Anuradha, 7. Jeyshta, 8. Moola.

The paryaya value of the husband's lunar Nashatra to building Nakshtra has the value of 8. Referring to the paryaya table below, we see that the paryaya value of 8 gives the benefit of "friendship." This is acceptable. The Nakshatra of the structure will have the positive influence of friendship on the husband. We accept this Nakshatra for the structure so far.

Applying this exercise to all members of the family to live in the structure:

Mother: Poorva Phalguni, *Paryaya value = 9 (supreme friendship)*
Father: Krithika, *paryaya value = 8 (friendship)*
Daughter One: Uttara Ashada, *paryaya value = 8 (friendship)*
Daughter Two: Satabhish, *paryaya value = 5 (neutral) See below for further comment*

Son: Chitra, *paryaya value = 6 (beneficial)*
Grandfather: Krithika, *paryaya value = 8 (friendship)*
Grandmother: Purnavasu, *paryaya value = 4 (welfare)*

Regarding Daughter Two: She has come up with a paryaya value of 5 (neutral). Normally a paryaya value of 5 is not accepted. However, if the 5 value falls in the third round of counting of the Nakshatra stars, it is accepted for most household members, but, *not for the wife.* In this example, Moola is the 5 relationship position in the third counting: *first round*: 1. Satabhish, 2. Poorva Bhad, 3. Uttara Bhad, 4. Revati, 5. Ashwini, 6. Bharai, 7. Krithika, 8. Rohini, 9. Mrigishira; *second round*: 1. Aridra, 2. Purnavasu, 3. Pushyami, 4. Aslesha, 5. Makha, 6. Poorva Phalguni, 7. Uttara Phalguni, 8. Hasta, 9. Chitra; *third round*: 1. Swati, 2. Vishaka, 3. Anuradha, 4. Jeyshta, 5. Moola.

At this point we have determined that the Nashatra Moola is beneficial for the whole family in terms of harmony between occupants and structure. We have eliminated Mrigishira because it was not beneficial for the husband. It is not likely that we will always be able to find a Nakshatra that is beneficial for all the family. We always start with finding a Nakshatra that is beneficial for the wife, at least, and hopefully the husband. If we cannot find something beneficial for the children, it is acceptable.

Step six:
We will carry the investigation of Ayadi value for 107, as well as 112, further for illustration's sake, even though we have thrown out any consideration of using 112 for the structure.

Formula two: yoni (direction or orientation) = Ayadi number x ⅜

The yoni calculation gives a value for the preferred orientation or the facing of the structure. There are eight directions to be considered:

Yoni table (direction)

1) Dwajam (flagstaff), east
2) Dhoomam (smoke), southeast
3) Simham (lion), south
4) Svanam (dog), southwest
5) Vrushabha (bull), west
6) Kharam (ass), northwest
7) Gajam (elephant), north
8) Kakam (crow), northeast

Directions that are accepted as good, having applied the Ayadi calculation, are Dwajam (east), Simham (south), Vrushabha (west) and Gajam (north). A structure cannot face any of the intermediate directions. It can face only the cardinal directions, east, south, west, and north.

Applying the yoni calculation of ⅜ to 112 and 107:

Example A: 112 x ⅜ = 336/8 = 42, with no fractional remainder. Therefore, the yoni value of 112 is 8 = Kakam (northeast). Kakam is not accepted as a Vastu compliant orientation. Another example: if we had take the number 111 x ⅜ = 333/8 = 41⅝, the remainder value of this number is 5 = Vrushabha (west). This direction would be accepted as a good yoni value for our example family because they will have an east-facing house. (See rules below for explanation on this.)

Example B: 107 x ⅜ = 321/8 = 40⅛. The fractional remainder is 1. The yoni value of 1 is Dwajam (east). This is perfect for our example client. We will accept this value and continue to test the merits of 107 as the mandala frequency.

The yoni value given by the calculation is called sthana yoni. It is number based. The yoni value given to the house by taking a reading on its facing is called dissa yoni. Once we calculate the sthana yoni (calculation based) we can then analyze the possible acceptable directions that the actual structure can face, the dissa yoni.

Here are the basic rules for sthana yoni versus dissa yoni:
1) If sthana yoni is Dwajam (east), the facing of the house can be east, south, or west.
2) If sthana yoni is Simham (south), the facing of the house can be south or east.
3) If sthana yoni is Vrushabham (west), the facing of the house can be west, east, or north.
4) If sthana yoni is Gajam (north), the facing of the house can be north or east.

The general influences of the facing of the house are 1) east: physical comfort and mental peace, 2) south: salvation and freedom from worldly desires, 3) west: material prosperity, 4) north: money, wealth.

A south-facing house is accepted for a good facing; however, the orientation to south is best for someone who is not very interested in worldly matters or comforts but more interested in spiritual liberation. In practice it is preferred to give the structure an east, north, or west orientation so that the occupants will have material abundance as well as psychological and spiritual comfort.

Once the investigation of the direction or orientation of the facing of the house is undertaken, the Vastu designer must keep in mind the actual site of the structure: which orientation will be allowed on the site in terms of practical considerations.

Step seven:
Third and fourth Ayadi calculations: income versus expenditure.

This investigation will give us an understanding if the influence of the mandala of the house will facilitate gain or loss of general prosperity of the occupants. Prosperity is a natural consequence of living in a Vastu-compliant house. Prosperity, in general, is the result of living in harmony with the laws of nature. Prosperity can be obtained by nefarious means also, but prosperity blended with peace of mind and heart will be the result of the Vastu environment.

Formula three: income (aayam) = Ayadi number x 8/12
Formula four: expenditure (vyayam) = Ayadi number x 9/10

Example A:
Aayam: 112 x 8/12 = 896/12 = 74 8/12 value = 8
Vyayam: 112 x 9/10 = 1008/10 = 100 8/10 value = 8
In this example income and expenditure are equal. The influence of the house will be neutral in terms of prosperity.

Example B:
Aayam: 107 x 8/12 = 856/12 = 71 4/12 value = 4
Vyayam: 107 x 9/10 = 963/10 = 96 3/10 value = 3
In this example income is 4 and expenditure is 3, the difference is 1. The influence of the house will be positive in terms of prosperity. The basic result we are looking for is to have the aayam value be greater that the vyayam value. The amount of the difference between the two values is of no significance. For example, if aayam is 5 and vyayam is 1 (a difference of 4), there is no greater prosperity available than the result of Example B above.

Step eight:
The next formula we check in the Sadayadi group of six formulas is varam, which means "week."

Formula five: varam = Ayadi number x 9/7.

Varam table
1. Sunday
2. Monday
3. Tuesday
4. Wednesday

5. Thursday
6. Friday
7. Saturday

The only days *not acceptable* for the house are Tuesday and Saturday.

Example A:
112 x 9/7 = 1008/7 = 144, no remainder (this indicates a 7 value). Value 7 (Saturday)
This is not accepted for a Vastu structure.
Example B:
107 x 9/7 = 963/7 = 137 4/7 = Remainder 4 (Wednesday) This value is acceptable for a Vastu structure.
Number 107 is looking good so far. Number 112 is not.

Step nine:
Amsam is the next and final formula of the Sadayadi group. Amsam means "quality." Amsam determines another layer of energy in the house that is a basic quality of the influence.

Formula six: amsam = Ayadi number x 4/9.

Amsam table:

1. Taskara: thief
2. Bhukti: enjoyment
3. Sakti: power
4. Dhanyam: blessed
5. Nrupan: king
6. Kleepan: neutral
7. Nirbheeti: fearlessness
8. Daridran: poor
9. Preshiyan: servant (In Sakaladhikara this aspect is accepted as good.)

Qualities 2,3,4,5,7, and 9 are accepted as good for a Vastu structure.

Example A:
112 x 4/9 = 448/9 = 49 7/9. Value = 7, nirbheeti (fearlessness). This is acceptable for a Vastu structure.
Example B:
107 x 4/9 = 428/9 = 47 5/9. Value = 5, nrupan (king). This is acceptable for a Vastu structure.

Summary of sample Ayadi investigation for the Smith family project:

Example A: #112

1. Nakshatra: Mrigishira
Good for wife, daughter two, and grandmother.
Not good for husband, daughter one, son, and grandfather.

2. Yoni: kakam (crow)
Not acceptable for a Vastu structure.

3. Aayam: 8

4. Vyayam: 8
Neutral value. Not acceptable for a Vastu structure.

5. Varam: Saturday
Not acceptable for a Vastu structure.

6. Amsam: nirbheeti (fearlessness)
Acceptable for a Vastu structure.

At this point the Vastu designer would determine that 112 is not an acceptable Ayadi number for the structure. All six formulas need to have a positive value for the number to be accepted.

Example B - #107

1. Nakshatra: Moola
Good for whole family.

2. Yoni: Dwajam (flagstaff)
Acceptable for a Vastu structure.

3. Aayam: 4

4. Vyayam: 3
Acceptable for a Vastu structure.

5. Varam: Wednesday
Acceptable for a Vastu structure.

6. Amsam: nrupan (king)
Acceptable for a Vastu structure.

Now it has become evident that Ayadi number 107 will be good for this project.

Age of the house

Along with the six formulas of the Sadayadi group, the age of the house must also be considered. "Age of the house" means the lifespan of the house: how long the house will be energized as a structure. The question arises, "What happens to the house when the lifespan is finished?" It may be possible to re-energize a structure and extend the lifespan. This is done with temples that have stood for thousands of years in India. These structures have remained alive and vibrant through the centuries. The exact science and technology is not available in this book.

Formula for lifespan of the house: Ayadi number x 27 ÷ 100.

Example A:
112 x 27 = 3,024 ÷ 100 = 30 24/100. Value = 24 years

Example B:
107 x 27 = 2,889 ÷ 100 = 28 89/100. Value = 89 years

A desirable age for a structure is fifty years or more.
An acceptable age for a house is thirty years or more. (Use these criteria only if you have no other choice.)

Example B shows that 107 remains a good Ayadi number for the Smith family.

Ayadi calculation tables

In common practice Vastu designers use an Ayadi calculation table of pre-worked formulas. In this table the six, ten, and sixteen formula sets are already imposed on numbers one to ten thousand. This allows the Vastu designer to bypass the work of running all the formulas each time. One simply runs down the list of positive Ayadi numbers and chooses an option. Below are some Ayadi values commonly used.

AYADI NUMBERS FOR VASTU PROJECTS

AYADI #	NAKSHATRA	YONI	AAYAM/VYAYAM	VARAM	AMSAM
37	26 Uttara Bhad	North	8/3	Wednesday	Dhanyam
39	15 Swati	West	12/1	Sunday	Sakti
55	8 Pushyami	West	8/5	Thursday	Dhanyam
59	13 Hasta	East	4/1	Friday	Bhukti
73	17 Anuradha	South	8/7	Friday	Dhanyam
85	5 Mrigishira	North	8/5	Monday	Nirbheeti
107	19 Moola	East	4/3	Wednesday	Nrupan
111	24 Satabhish	West	12/9	Thursday	Sakti
129	6 Aridra (Tiru)	South	12/1	Friday	Sakti
139	5 Mrigishira	East	8/1	Thursday	Nirbheeti
165	24 Satabhish	North	12/5	Sunday	Sakti
199	26 Uttara Bhad	West	8/1	Friday	Dhanyam
237	6 Aridra (Tiru)	North	12/3	Thursday	Sakti
239	22 Sravana	West	4/1	Monday	Bhukti
247	5 Mrigishira	West	8/3	Wednesday	Nirbheeti
255	15 Swati	West	12/5	Friday	Sakti
265	14 Chitra	South	8/5	Thursday	Nirbheeti
269	19 Moola	North	4/1	Friday	Nrupan
291	6 Aridra (Tiru)	East	12/9	Sunday	Sakti

■ What you learned in this chapter:

1) Ayadi calculations are the ancient formulas used to define the dimensions of the Vastu structure such that it can resonate with the occupant and the Earth and cosmic energy matrices.

2) The main factor in determining resonance is the "birth star," or lunar Nakshatra, of the organism.

3) Each birth star carries a unique vibration and influence and Ayadi formulas are used to understand these influences to create balance and harmony.

4) The birth star of the structure is related to the perimeter value of the Vastu Purusha Mandala of the structure.

5) There are six basic formulas used in Ayadi for secular structures but as many as sixteen can be used.

6) The life span of the structure is also calculated and considered in Vastu formulas.

8. Rectification: A Balancing Act

In my architecture practice, I receive hundreds of inquiries a year regarding existing buildings. Interest in Vastu architecture has increased greatly and people who already have real estate are wondering how their properties shape up to Vastu standards.

In general Vastu architecture principles are meant to be implemented from the ground up. In the Vastu discipline, we use formulas and principles that have been recognized as basic in the process of material manifestation from unified Source Energy.
Ideally we don't try to make the principles fit the building; instead, we make the building fit the principles. For predictable positive results, we need proper orientation, plan layout, mandala dimensions, and entry. These are the basics, and they are very difficult to find in existing structures.

Vastu science does not have a prescribed technology of rectification. *To be clear, no technology, such as placement of yantras or other sacred objects, can be prescribed by Vastu science for the rectification of negative aspects in a structure.* Such measures may have some value in terms of improving the energy in an environment, but they are not a part of the Vastu technology. *The process of rectification of existing buildings is purely experimental.* If it is our only choice, we can try to apply certain principles to clean up the energy of the structure. With experience a Vastu designer can sometimes achieve something positive with a rectification.

It is important to keep in mind that the building is a living organism. We must treat it with a respect similar to any living being. I recommend that if you undertake a renovation of any kind, you treat the building as gently as a doctor would a patient. You could go as far as having a "talk" of some sort with the building before construction. Explain the purpose of the intrusions. Also, keep the building environment neat and orderly.

It's my opinion that negative elements in a non-Vastu structure have a less negative effect, because the structure itself is not highly energized with Earth and cosmic energies. The non-Vastu house is a poor conductor of energy. A Vastu house would conduct these energies as if they were gold. A non-Vastu house would be like wood in terms of electrical conductance.

Some structures take very little analysis in terms of Vastu to understand that they are not a good environment. Trust your intuition in this matter. If you walk into a structure and you feel a loss of energy or oppressed or confused, then avoid it whenever possible.

One important point on this: Don't live in fear of a building. Fear can be more destructive that any building space. The human nervous system is also a Vastu structure. If you own a structure that is non-compliant and cannot shift elsewhere, use your own pure energy to bless and consecrate the structure. If, apart from any Vastu considerations, you have a natural feeling that you don't like your home or office, then, when possible, find a way to relocate to a space that is more satisfying for you. If you can't move, try to foster a positive relationship with the structure.

Here are some suggestions on how to improve your relationship with the structure:

1) Keep your space clean and orderly.

2) Have a ritual cleaning at least once a month. This could be something like going through the house with sage or sandalwood smoke.

3) Speak to the structure: treat it like the living being that it is. Remember, an enclosed space vibrates with life. Tell the structure that you are grateful for the shelter it gives. You might even name the house. Choose a name that suits its character and makes you happy.

4) Fill the atmosphere of the house with soothing and healing scents by using aroma oils and incense. Also, uplifting music should be played regularly in the space, even when you are not present to hear it. Carnatic music is one good choice for uplifting music.

5) Decorate the space with furniture, art and colors that you love. Even one room fixed up to perfection will make a big difference. This room can be your haven within the non-compliant home.

6) Place something sacred and uplifting at the entry of the structure so that each time you enter you will be reminded of the truth of inner peace and unity of life. Deep within our heart center is the primal Vastu structure that vibrates life to every cell, to every sacred center of the body. No matter where we live, our own Vastu energy can fill our environment with peace and energy.

Basic Considerations in Rectification:

Gathering the data

Site analysis

Gather this information to present to your Vastu architect:

1. plot map and orientation to true north
2. direction of downward slope of land (if any)
3. description of any water on or near the site:
    o what type of water is it? (pond, stream, spring, lake, river, etc.)
    o how far is the water source from the proposed house site
    o what size is the body of water?
    o In the case of a river, location and direction of flow are important.
4. location and type of any outstanding landscape features
5. location of adjacent houses and streets
6. location of any public buildings or other neighborhood features

Orientation

The first consideration in rectification is orientation. We must analyze the relationship of the building to the cardinal points of the compass. We determine the direction of true north with respect to the building and arrive at a clear understanding of the orientation of the structure. Good orientation means the building is not rotated more than ten degrees away from true north/south/east/west. Ideally the rotation is not more than three degrees. Rotation from true north more than ten degrees creates a building that will not be resonant enough with the Earth energy grid to give the Vastu effect. If a building is rotated more than ten degrees, in general it should be rejected for consideration in a Vastu rectification.

For an east- and west-facing building, rotation can be counterclockwise, not clockwise. This means an east-facing building is turned slightly toward the north and a west-facing building is turned slightly toward the south. For a north- and south-facing building, rotation can be clockwise, not counterclockwise. This means a north-facing building is turned slightly toward the east and a south-facing building is turned slightly toward the west.

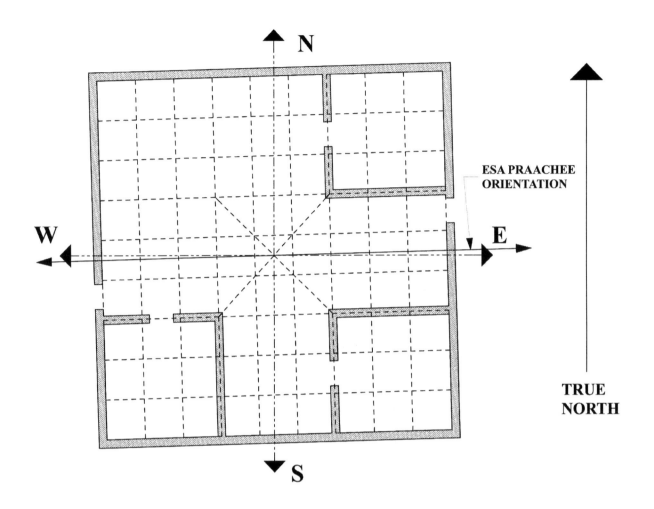

Illustration 72
East or west facing building
is rotated 1.5 degrees
counter-clockwise

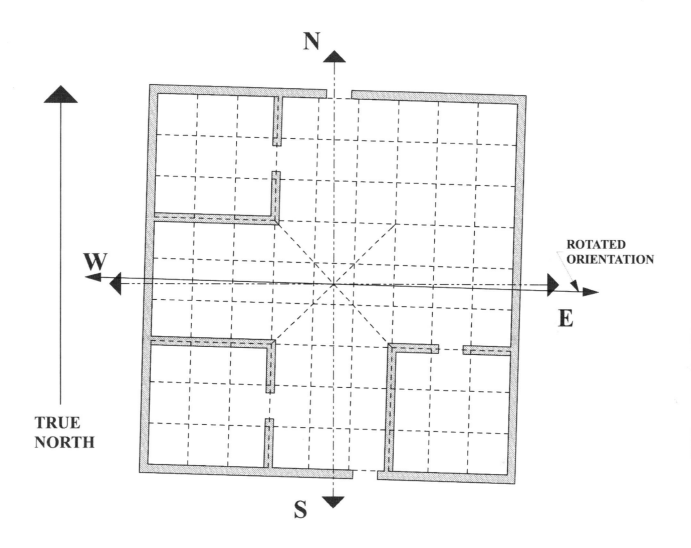

Illustration 73
North or south facing building
is rotated 1.5 degrees clockwise

True north

We use true north (not magnetic north) to judge the orientation of the existing building. Sometimes the owner will have a surveyor's plot map that shows the exact orientation of the structure. If you have such a map, be sure it is an official survey and not an informal plot map. Sometimes informal plot maps will indicate a general direction of north and not true north.

If you don't have a surveyors map, the first step in determining the orientation of the building is to find out what the magnetic declination is at your site location. Magnetic declination is the difference between magnetic north (the direction the compass indicates is north) and true north (the direction along the Earth's surface toward the geographic north pole). Declination is a very important issue in determining orientation because in some areas a large difference exists between magnetic north and true north. In Maine, for example, the declination is twenty degrees west. This means the north arrow on the compass points twenty degrees to the west of true north.

In using a compass, you must be careful to avoid local magnetic influences. Hold the compass off the ground and keep it away from the building and any electrical lines or machinery or mechanical systems, such as water pipes. A half-inch thick piece of rigid plywood about two feet by two feet can be used as a standoff for the compass. Place the compass on the outer edge of the plywood; then place the plywood against the building in *several* areas (to confirm the reading) to find magnetic north. This procedure holds the compass about two feet away from the building. Once magnetic north is determined, do the simple math needed to understand the direction of true north.

Slope of the land

Analysis should be done for the slope of the land around the building and also for the general land mass in the geographic area. Simply put, we want the land around the structure to be flat or gently sloping to east, northeast, north and/or northwest. These conditions have positive influences. It is not advisable to attempt to rectify a negative condition by moving large quantities of earth to change a slope condition. The basic influences underlying the creation of the existing terrain are still present. It is possible to move a small amount of soil to create a flat area around a structure to be able to place a protecting Vastu fence around it. On the other hand, it is possible, with the help of a Vastu architect, to site a structure under specific conditions that are not perfectly compliant with Vastu prescriptions.

Ideally an existing structure under inspection for Vastu considerations should have a Vastu fence that helps contain the energy of the space. It may be possible for a Vastu consultant to create a Vastu fence that will have good resonance with the mandala of the structure.

Nature influences: water, rocks, mountains, trees, sunrise, rivers, etc.

Location of a water body near the structure is significant. The ideal location for water will be to the northeast. However, the water body should not be in a position such that when we extend the centerline of the mandala of the structure this line crosses into it.

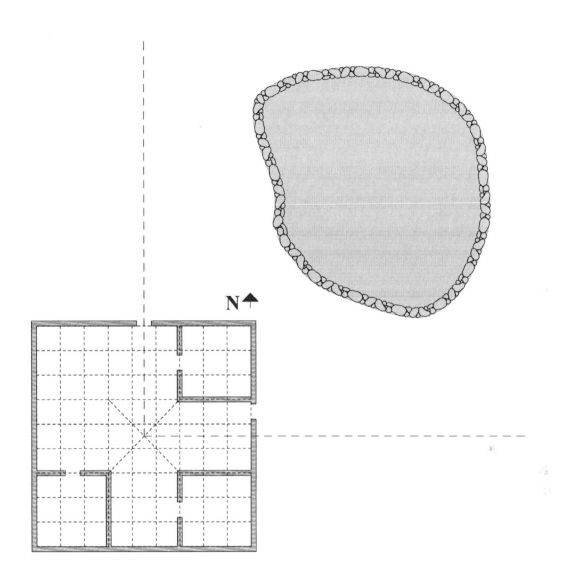

Illustration 74
Body of water located in an
auspicous position: northeast
of the structure

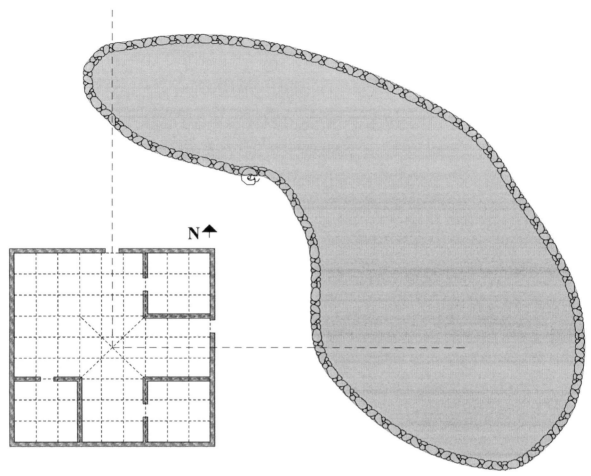

Illustration 75
Body of water located in a
less than desirable position due
to extension of the water across
the centerlines of the house

The size of the water body is significant. A small pond has less influence than a lake or river or sea. Water located in areas other than the northeast should be at least one thousand feet away from the structure. The chapter on site selection outlines the requirements for an ideal Vastu site. Use this chapter as a checklist for all site analysis.

Front door location and the mandala of the structure

Once the orientation of the structure has been established, we can identify the facing direction. The face of the house is the front of the house: where the front door is. (For example, as you walk out the front door of the structure, if you are facing east, the structure is an east-facing structure.) If the front door as described above is on the east, but the door the owner uses the most is on the north side of the structure, the facing of the house is still considered to be to the east. This east door location is then analyzed in terms of the mandala of the structure.

The location of the main entry door will usually be obvious. It is this location that defines the front of the structure. Sometimes the direction the main door faces does not define the facing of the house. If the front door is located on the South side (for example), but the entry door faces East on the South side, this is still defined as a South entrance.

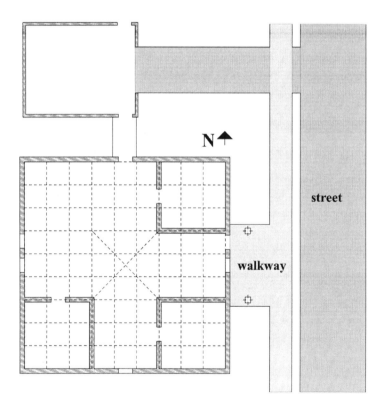

Illustration 76
East facing building with
secondary north entry

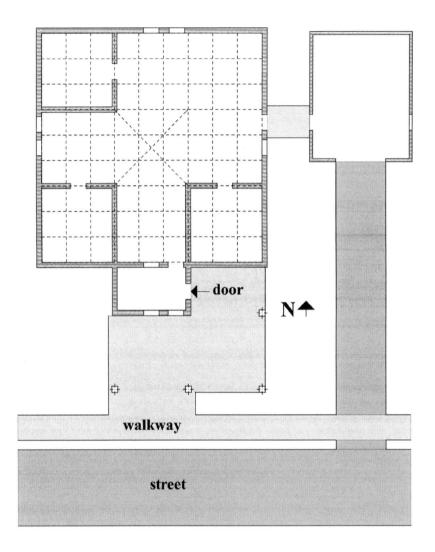

Illustration 77
South facing building with an east facing
door on the south side: this is considered a
south entrance

To evaluate the position of the main entry door, we must establish an opinion of the main geometric mandala of the building by doing an analysis of the possible mandalic geometry of the floor plan. This analysis is done because sometimes it is possible to try for a relocation of the main entry door for a more auspicious effect. If the existing door is in a location that is not auspicious, we can move the door within the same side of the building, or we can change the main entry to another side of the building. For example, if the house faces south and the main door is in the center south location, we can shift the door to a better location in the south wall or choose another existing door or create a new door on the east or west or north wall.

Considerations for this type of rectification: (These are considerations to try for)

I want to emphasize that this design change for rectification is purely experimental. *A non-Vastu house is usually a low energy house and rectification solutions can be of little effect. It is even possible to make a change for the worse. For rectification a Vastu expert must be engaged.*

1) The new door must be the largest entry door of the house.

2) Location of the new door: It must be placed with respect to the mandala we have created for the house, in an auspicious location. Placing the new door just anywhere will have no chance of creating a beneficial effect.

3) Location of the door with respect to the floor plan: The new door location must take into consideration the interior wall configuration. The door should open in such a way as to allow good flow of energy into the house. An axis of sight through the house leading to a window or door in the opposite side of the house is desirable.

4) Location of the door with respect to the site: The new door should not be obstructed by a large object, such as a large tree trunk or rock, immediately opposite the opening.

5) Location of the door should not be ridiculous: The house needs to maintain aesthetic value. The design must suit the house.

If the existing structure does not have a regular and simple geometry, analyzing the mandala can be a difficult prospect. We are looking for the dominant geometrical shape of the building. Specifically, we are looking for a more regular shape of a square or a rectangle. The dominant geometry may best be represented by the main exterior walls of the house that support the main and largest body of roof. Below is an example of a mandala analysis on a non-Vastu structure.

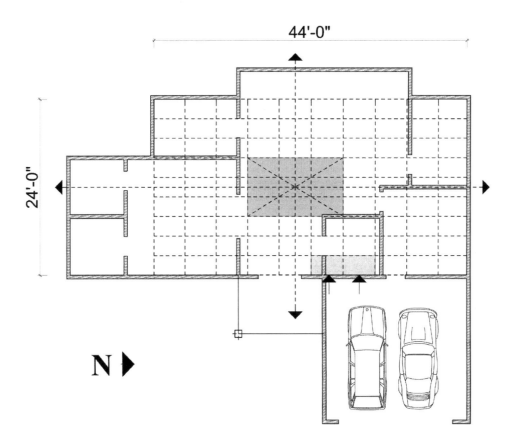

Illustration 78
Mandala "A"
Perimeter value - 136'

As you can see, attempting to apply a Vastu mandala to an existing house is a less than perfect science. Several mandalas may apply to the structure. The best we can do is to choose a mandala that seems correct. Sometimes the geometry of the mandala is obvious: the floor plan may be a simple geometric shape, like a rectangle or square. If the floor plan does not have a simple geometry, we need to lay out all the possible mandalas and then do a careful analysis.

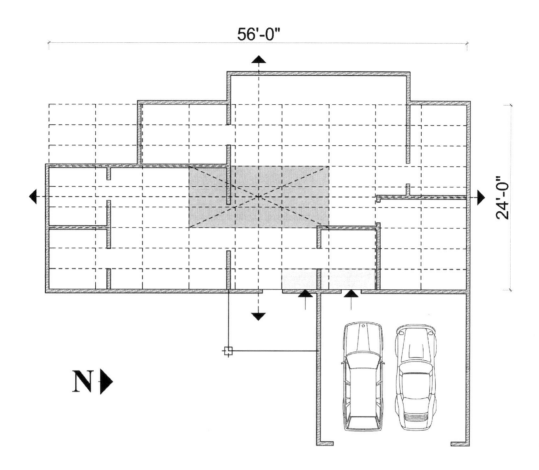

Illustration 79
Mandala "B"
Perimeter value - 160'

Under these conditions the Vastu consultant is still working on purely experimental solutions. The goal is to try to identify the dominant geometry of the plan of the structure. Different mandalas are laid over the floor plan and the pros and cons of each are considered. The designer looks for compliance with room locations, Brahmastan, wall positions, and exterior door locations. Also, the position of polluting elements—toilets, stairs, etc.—is considered. Ayadi calculations can be applied to the mandala and it may give some indication of the influence of the floor plan on the occupants.

Analysis of the floor plan examples above:

Mandala value in A

Perimeter value: 136'0"
136'0" ÷ 2'9" = 49.45 (hasta unit of measure)
136'0" ÷ 1'4½" = 98.90 (vitasti unit of measure)
136'0" ÷ 8 1/4" = 197.82 (taalam of measure)
The closest value to a whole unit in the perimeter is 99 (vitasti unit of measure). We take the 98.9 and round it to 99.

Mandala value B

Perimeter value: 160'0"
160'0" ÷ 2'-9" = 58.18 (hasta unit of measure)
160'0" ÷ 1'4½" = 116.36 (vitasti unit of measure)
136'0" ÷ 8¼" = 232.73 (taalam unit of measure)

The closest value to a whole unit in the perimeter is 233 (taalam unit of measure). We take the 232.73 and round it to 233.

As you see, analysis for rectification is not an exact science. A compromise is usually involved.

Note: This perimeter value in the example is measured to the inside face of finished wall. This is the first value we check when measuring the perimeter dimension. We can also take the dimension of the outside of exterior wall or middle of exterior wall. A deep analysis of the mandala value of an existing building may require this detailed measuring. In our example A, if we take the exterior wall as 8" thick from face of interior to face of exterior, then there are 3 possible perimeter values: 1) Inside face of exterior wall = 44' + 44' + 24' + 24' = 136'0"; 2) Outside face of exterior wall = 45'4"+ 45'4" + 24'4" + 25'4" = 141'4"; 3) Middle of exterior wall = 44'8"+ 44'8" + 24'8" + 24'8" = 138'8". Once we have all these perimeter values, we can submit them to the Ayadi formulas and study the values we find. By doing this in-depth analysis, it may be possible to see all the effects of a potential building mandala.

Applying a mandala to a non-Vastu building is a flawed procedure in that the non-Vastu building does not resonate with strong energy like a Vastu building. Even if we find a mandala that seems to work for the building and for what has been the experience of the occupants of the building, we must realize that we are only speculating. However, when an analysis of an existing building is a mandate for a client, we can go through these complicated procedures and report on what might be happening with the building.

I have used this type of analysis with success on non-Vastu and Vastu buildings. One client I had was considering moving into a "Vastu" office building. On the surface, the design had followed many Vastu principles. It had a wonderful Brahmastan open to the sky, and the entry, orientation, and layout seemed good. However, on further analysis I found the building was flawed. I suggested to the client that his business and health might have challenges if he occupied the building. Eventually the client did occupy a large part of the building, ignoring my recommendation. Within one year the client came to me and told me that everything I had warned of had transpired!

Analysis of Ayadi value of 99 and 233 for the illustration:

1) Nakshatra: formula = 8/27
99 x 8/27 = remainder of 9: Aslesha
233 x 8/27 = remainder of 1: Ashwini

Application of paryaya table effects for a client with Rohini birthstar:
99: paryaya value = 6: Sadhakam (beneficial effects)
233: paryaya value = 7: Vadham (death)
In this example, obviously, the 233 mandala value will not have beneficial effects.

2) Yoni: formula = ⅜
99 x ⅜ = remainder of 1 (Dwajam: east)
233 x ⅜ = remainder of 3 (Simham: south)

Both values are beneficial. However, we must consider the orientation—east—of the structure in consideration. An east-facing structure can accept both east and south yoni values.

3) Income (aayam) versus expenditure (vyayam): formulas 8/12 and 9/10, respectively
99 x 8/12 = remainder of 12
99 x 9/10 = remainder of 1

233 x 8/12 = remainder of 4
233 x 9/10 = remainder of 7
In this case 99 is positive for gain but 233 is not.

4) Varam: formula = 9/7
99 x 9/7 = remainder of 2 (Monday)
233 x 9/7 = remainder of 4 (Wednesday)
Both values are positive.

5) Amsam: formula = 4/9

99 x 4/9 = remainder of 9 (servant)

233 x 4/9 = remainder of 5 (king)

In general, both values are acceptable; however "servant" is less auspicious.

Based on our investigation with Ayadi and observation of the existing conditions of the structure, we may ask some questions of the occupants, but only if they have occupied the building for some time. It would probably be better if occupancy has been longer than a year (four seasons). The questions should not "lead the witness." We don't want to put words in the client's mouth. If we see the possibility of some problem created by the floor plan, we can ask some simple and non-biased questions. Ask general questions about their health, income, emotional state, etc., and allow them to answer without any influence from your side.

Remember, it is very difficult to predict the effect of a building with little or no compliance to Vastu principles. If we do find the building has some compliance, then we can form a gentle opinion on its energetic effect.

For example, if we find one of the children has a bedroom in the southeast corner (Fire element influence), we could ask if any of the children has a temperament challenge. We ask about the children in general so we don't alarm them about the child in the southeast bedroom in particular. Sleeping in the southeast may bring the influence of too much Fire energy. This could cause heat in the temperament. In a non-Vastu house, this is not a given, it is just a possibility. If we discover the person in the southeast bedroom is temperamental, we can suggest a room change. This is one example of a very simple, *experimental*, adjustment that could be tried to respond to Vastu requirements.

For general rectification considerations, the general points are:

1) The best location for the kitchen is in the southeast with the cook facing east to cook. If the cook can be on the east wall and not the center of the kitchen, it is ideal.

2) Master bedroom can be in southwest or south with top of head board of bed to the east or south. This means the person sleeps with the top of the head to east or south.

3) Meditation or shrine room in the northeast with Gods facing east.

4) Other bedrooms can be in the north, northwest (best for guests or elder child), west, east, south, and northeast (best for elders or brahmachari).

5) Not suitable for sleeping: center of house and southeast.

6) Bathrooms, especially toilets, should not be on the centerline of the house in either direction or on the diagonal lines from the southeast to northwest and southwest to northeast.

7) Stairs should not be on the diagonal lines from the southeast to northwest and southwest to northeast.

8) The dining area is good in the west, southeast, and south. However, location of dining is fairly flexible in general.

9) An office for ladies should be in the southwest or east.

10) The center of the house should be left open and free of walls. a) It can be used as a room for sitting but not for working, cooking, a toilet, or sleeping. If the center, Brahmastan, is obstructed or non-existent, the energy of the structure will be very low and any other remedial effort will be affected negatively. At least, the very center of the mandala that we have chosen for the structure should be clear of obstruction. b) The Brahmastan should have sky light coming from above at least at the top most floor. c) Mechanical systems, such as heating or air conditioning, should not be in the center of the structure.
Anything placed in the mandala will influence the energy of the whole house. For example, if the Brahmastan has a fountain in it, water energy will be influencing the whole house. This is not recommended for the health of the occupants.

11) Fireplaces that are frequently used should not be in corners (except southeast) and should not fall on centerlines of the house. The best location for a fire is in the southeast area of the house.

Once we have a Vastu mandala laid over the plan of the house, we will have a picture of how well the walls of the house come into resonance with it. Resonance with the mandala means the walls fall on the grid lines of the mandala. Ideally the relationship to the grid line is to center of wall or to either side of the face of finished wall. In most existing modern structures, a high percentage of resonance is absent. Doing this exercise with the floor plan illustrates the challenges of rectification.

If we have a simple structure, it may be possible to make a change in the measurement of the mandala we choose for the structure. We can use Ayadi calculations to choose a beneficial mandala and thicken the wall as required to create the proper space.

Once we have given the structure a mandala, we can check the location of the front door and evaluate the prescribed influences of the entry location. We use the standard nine-by-nine mandala and check what the standard influence is for the door location. In illustration #80 the existing front door is located in the center and south of center module of the VPM. This location is not auspicious, and it would be good to attempt to relocate the front door if possible.

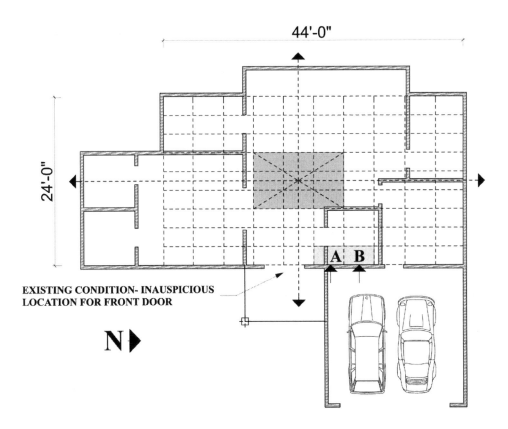

Illustration 80
Mandala "A"
Perimeter value - 136'
Relocate main entry door to module A or B

Room location:

Once we apply the mandala to the building, we can also evaluate it for room locations. We look for compliance with the basic important rooms: kitchen (southeast), master bedroom (southwest or south), meditation or puja (northeast), Brahmastan (center).

In general we can take the basic elemental influences of the mandala location and comment on what might be the effect in the family. If, for example, we find the master bedroom falling in the southeast corner of the house, we will need to advise the client that it is not an ideal location for rest and rejuvenation. As stated above, southeast is an area influenced by the Fire element and it may give too much heat to the person who tries to rest there. If we find the youngest child's bedroom in the southwest, we can advise that the child might be a dominate energy in the household. Southwest is the place for the master of the house. If a child sleeps there, he may try to rule the roost.

Polluting influences within the mandala are stairs, bathrooms, and toilets. We can look at the location of these elements and see if they fall in the corners or center or on the diagonal or center lines of the mandala. Finding this, we point out possible negative influences.

Another major influence in a structure is the mechanical systems. These systems should not be located in the Brahmastan of the mandala of the building. Heating and air systems should be in the southeast or northwest of the building if possible.

Illustration #81 illustrates a floor plan with some problems. Such problems are typically found in modern buildings. Stair, fireplace, and toilet locations are likely to be placed in areas not accepted by Vastu principles. Please review this plan as an example of a non-compliant house.

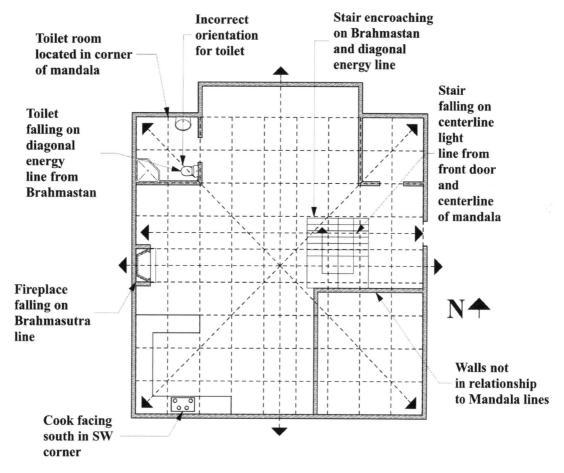

Illustration 81
Example of a non-compliant home

Creating a new sacred space within the existing non-compliant space

A Vastu structure creates a space that has specific geometry, dimensions, and beneficial effects. This carefully crafted space vibrates with a predictable energy that is good for the occupants. For an existing non-compliant building, as an experiment, we can create a perfect Vastu space within it. We can choose a room to dedicate to a Vastu mandala, and, in theory, the room will vibrate with good energy and influence the whole structure.

Ideally we choose a room that can conform perfectly to Vastu principles, including the entry to the room and the light axis in both directions. Below are some examples of creating a Vastu space within an existing space.

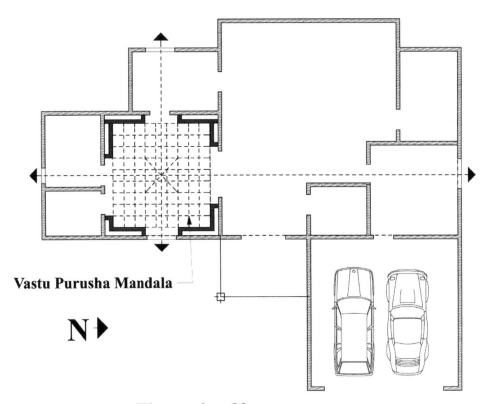

Vastu Purusha Mandala

N▶

Illustration 82
Creating a Vastu Purusha Mandala
within an existing structure

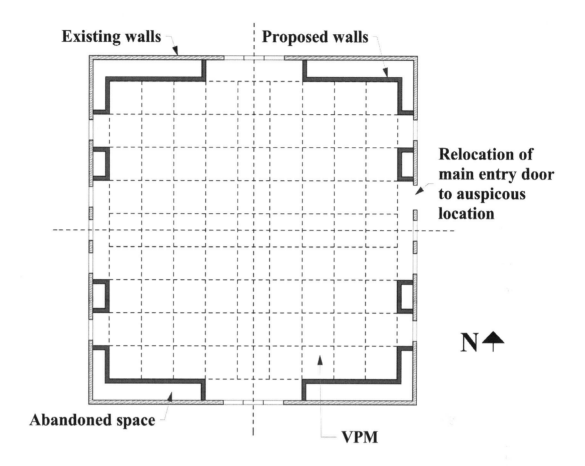

**Illustration 83
Creating a Vastu Purusha Mandala
by changing the interior space of
an existing building**

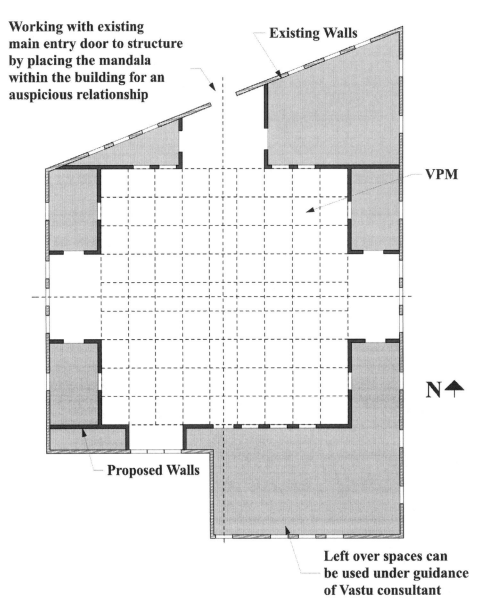

Working with existing main entry door to structure by placing the mandala within the building for an auspicious relationship

Existing Walls

VPM

N

Proposed Walls

Left over spaces can be used under guidance of Vastu consultant

Illustration 84
Creating a Vastu Purusha Mandala
within an existing irregular shaped structure

Another possible rectification solution with which to experiment is the addition of a Vastu shrine within the non-compliant structure or in the yard nearby the structure. The Vastu shrine is a perfect Vastu structure, usually of reduced scale. I have created small wooden shrines of perfect Vastu dimensions that stand about two feet tall. Being perfect in terms of geometry and dimension, the shrine will vibrate with Vastu energy. According to reports the healing energy waves of these shrines offer some relief for a building that in non-compliant.

I allowed this chapter on rectification because thousands of people have contacted me over the years desiring help with an existing structure. Please keep in mind that Vastu rectification is experimental. It should not be considered a first choice for someone who wants a fully compliant Vastu structure. There is no way to predict the effects of rectification. It is just to be used when no other choice is available.

Vastu checklist for project and rectification considerations

Basic considerations:
1) Orientation
2) Facing direction of structure
3) External elements—site-related
4) Vastu Purusha Mandala
5) Entry location
6) Room locations within the floor plan
7) Location of polluting elements within the structure
8) Vastu fence

The purpose of the Vastu checklist is to provide information for a Vastu evaluation. The results of this evaluation will give some indication of the condition of the structure (proposed or existing) in terms of Vastu science. The information collected should be given to a Vastu consultant to facilitate design considerations.

Orientation

Verify the exact orientation of the structure in terms of the cardinal points of the compass: north/south/east/west. Compute a value for the orientation; for example, the structure's front wall faces north but is rotated four and a half degrees toward northeast.

The structure will need to conform to the basic orientation requirements outlined in the chapter on orientation, or it will not be possible to apply Vastu principles for the Vastu effect.

Facing direction of the structure

The facing of the building is determined by the "front" of the building. With an existing structure, the front can be ambiguous. In general east, north, and west facings are best for residential structures.

External elements—site-related

Certain elements adjacent to the structure and the site can be problematic:

A) Street location is one of the most common issues: avoid a property that has a street that comes directly at the structure.

B) Water elements—lakes, rivers, seas, pools—should be located to the northeast area of the structure. The Vastu consultant can evaluate the particulars of water location, taking into consideration the exact condition of water not in the prescribed northeast location.

C) Landscape elements that fall on the extension of the lines of light of a structure are to be avoided. See page 18 for further information on this.

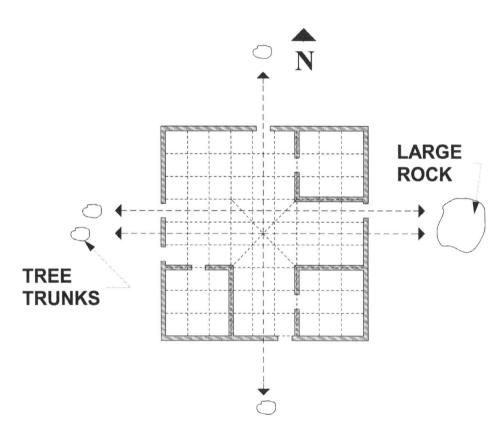

**Illustration 85 - Axis lines of structure
shall NOT be obstructed by landscape objects**

D) Sunrise obstruction: Avoid obstructions to the east of the structure that delay the morning sun rays from touching the house for several hours. A Vastu consultant would need to evaluate the condition.

Vastu Purusha Mandala

The geometry of the building should relate to a Vastu Purusha Mandala, the sacred geometry paradigm employed by Vastu science. In existing buildings the simpler the geometry the better: square or rectangular floor plans are preferred.

Entry location

The main entry should be on the facing side in the correct location as determined by assigning a Vastu Purusha Mandala for the structure.

Room locations within the floor plan

The basic requirements are that the

A) kitchen in the southeast with cook facing east;

B) the master bedroom is in the southwest or south, with a sleeping configuration such that the top of the head is to the east or south when lying down;

C) the puja or meditation room is in the northeast; and

D) the center of the structure should be free and open: Brahmastan.

Location of polluting elements within the structure

As a most basic requirement, toilets and stairs should not be in the corners or the center of the main room. There are many other considerations for polluting elements, but initial evaluation can begin with this observation.

Vastu fence
The structure should have a protecting "fence" or some landscape structure that contains the energy of the building.

■ **What you learned in this chapter:**

1) Vastu science does not have a prescribed technology of rectification.

2) Existing buildings present many challenges in terms of application of Vastu principles in rectification. The results will often be unpredictable.

3) For predictable results it is necessary to build from the ground up with Vastu principles.

4) A non-Vastu building may be a perfectly fine structure to occupy if one takes some simple steps to create a good atmosphere in the building. However, the Vastu effect will not be present.

5) In rectification some basic, necessary requirements need to be addressed. If these can be addressed, positive changes in the building environment may be possible.

6) Identifying a Vastu Purusha Mandala in the existing building geometry is an important factor in understanding the energetic influence of the structure.

7) Sometimes it is possible for an experienced Vastu practitioner to analyze the effects of an existing building—but not always!

8) One of the basic items to observe in an existing structure is the location of polluting or obstructing elements.

9) It may be possible to introduce a Vastu geometry in an existing structure, such as a shrine or newly dimensioned room within the structure that will bring in a Vastu influence.

9. Vastu House Plans

The plans presented can be used by builders if the orientation and all the dimensions are followed strictly as drawn and according to all the rules of this book on Vastu architecture. The noted dimensions of each floor plan must be strictly located to face of finished wall or center of wall as noted. "Face of finished wall" means the location of the wall surface once the final coating is placed on the wall: the coating that you can place your hand on when you are living in the house. Face of finished wall does NOT mean the location of the surface of the rough constructed structural wall. The author will publish a plan book on Vastu buildings in the future that will offer more and varied Vastu projects than can be built.

Plan "A" is suitable for occupants with the following lunar Nakshatras:

NAKSHATRA CHART FOR PLAN A		
Column 1	Column 2	Column 3
2-Bharai (Venus)	11-Poorva Phal (Venus)	20-Poorva Ashada (Venus)
3-Krithika (Sun)	12-Uttara Phal (Sun)	21-Uttara Ashada (Sun)
5-Mrigishira (Mars)	14-Chitra (Mars)	23-Dhanishta (Mars)
7-Purnavasu (Jupiter)	16-Vishaka (Jupiter)	25-Poorva Bhad (Jupiter)
9-Aslesha (Mercury)	18-Jeyshta (Kettai) (Mercury)	27-Revati (Mercury)

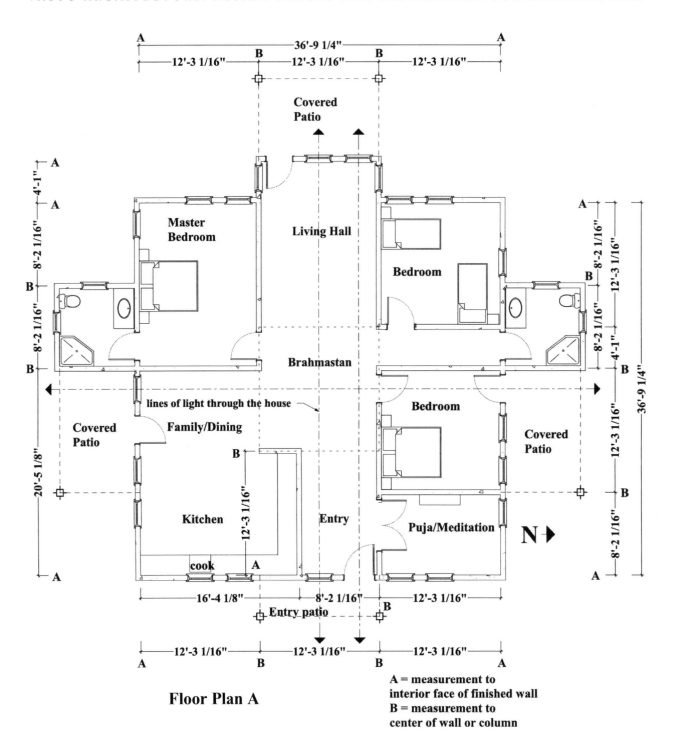

Floor Plan A

A = measurement to interior face of finished wall
B = measurement to center of wall or column

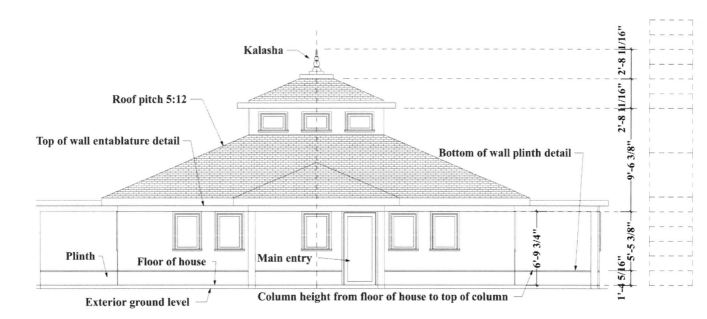

Plan A - East Elevation

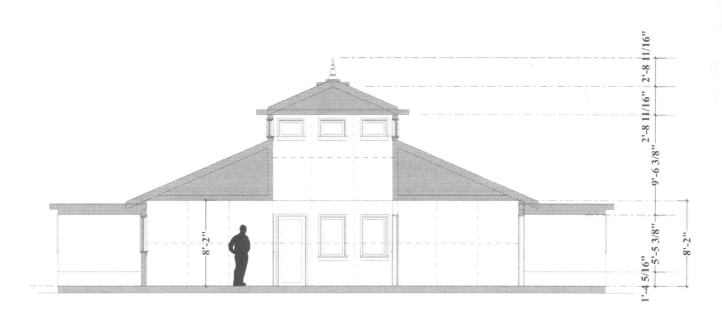

Plan A - Section - south/north - modulated space

NAKSHATRA CHART FOR PLAN B		
Plan "B" is suitable for occupants with the following lunar Nakshatras		
Column 1	Column 2	Column 3
1-Ashwini (Ketu)	10-Makha (Ketu)	19-Moola (Ketu)
2-Bharai (Venus)	11-Poorva Phal (Venus)	20-Poorva Ashada (Venus)
4-Rohini (Moon)	13-Hasta (Moon)	22-Sravana (Thiru) (Moon)
6-Aridra (Tiru) (Rahu)	15-Swati (Rahu)	24-Satabhish (Rahu)
8-Pushyami (Saturn)	17-Anuradha (Saturn)	26-Uttara Bhad (Saturn)

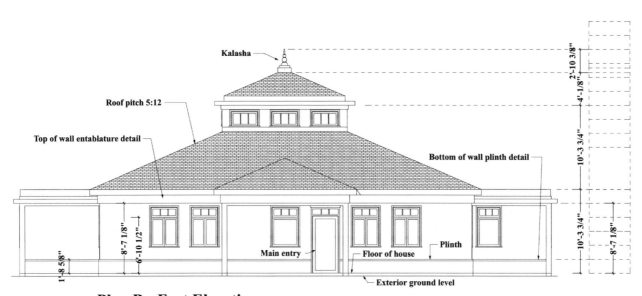

Plan B - East Elevation

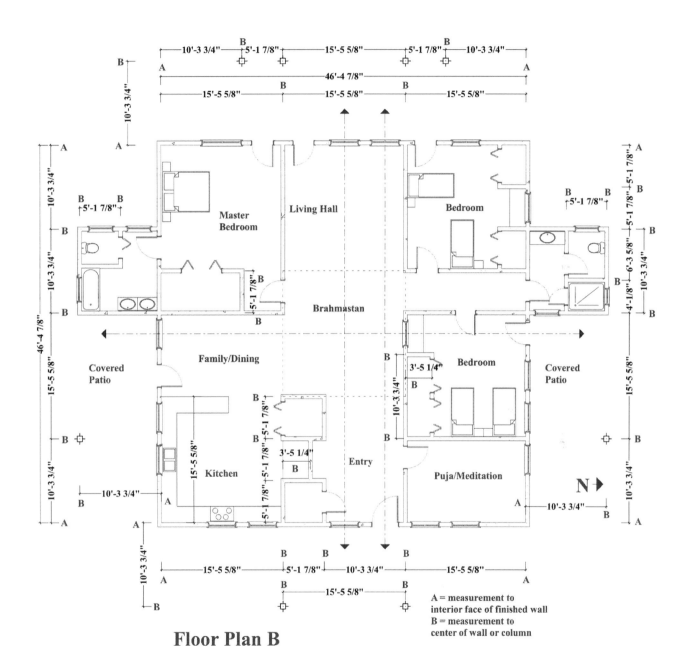

Floor Plan B

A = measurement to interior face of finished wall
B = measurement to center of wall or column

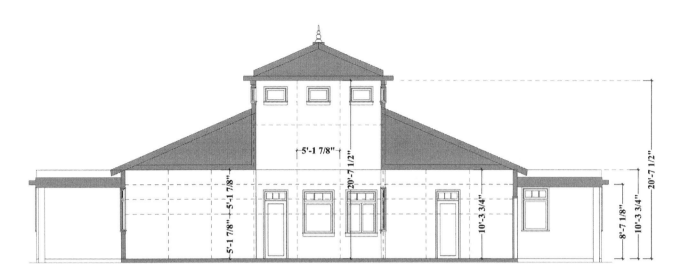

Plan B - Section - south/north - modulated space

Sample Vastu Projects

Family Home – East Elevation

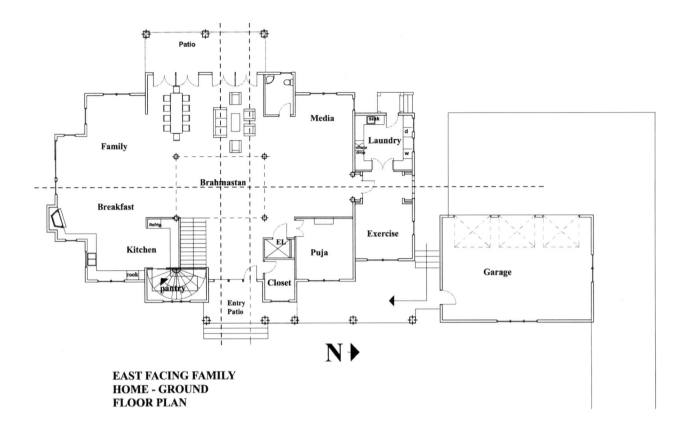

**EAST FACING FAMILY
HOME - GROUND
FLOOR PLAN**

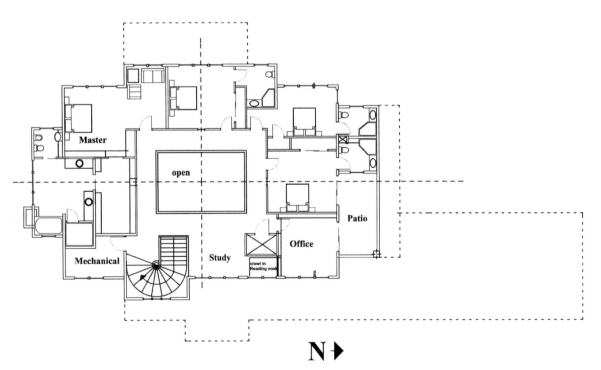

Family Home – 2nd Floor Plan

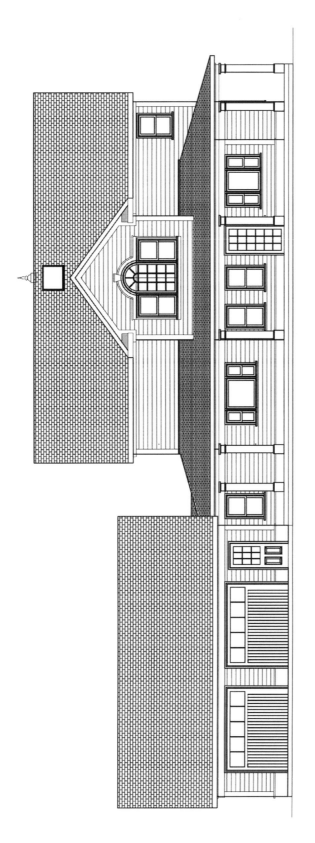

Country Home – East Elevation

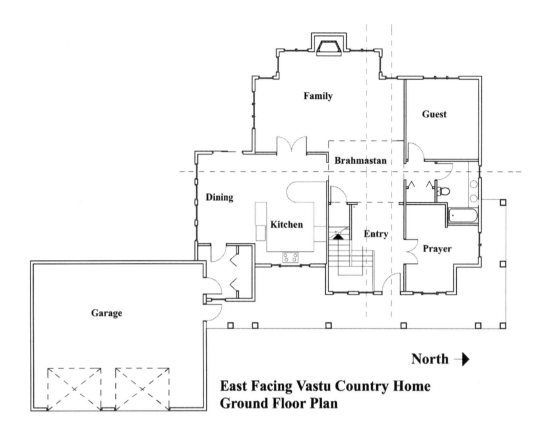

East Facing Vastu Country Home
Ground Floor Plan

Country Home – 2nd Floor Plan

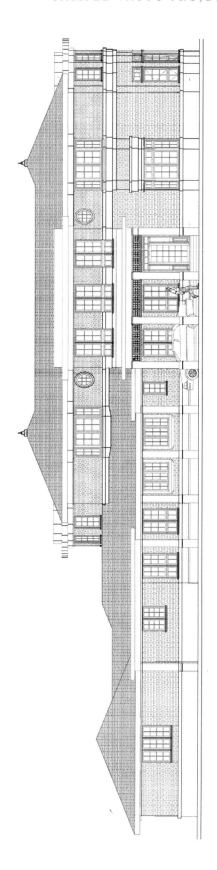

Villa Home – East Elevation

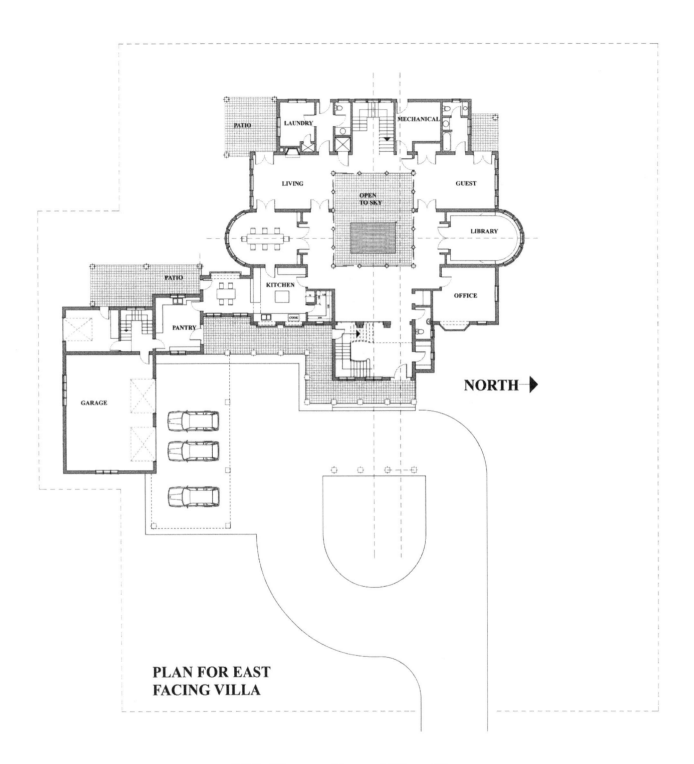

**PLAN FOR EAST
FACING VILLA**

Villa Home – Ground Floor Plan

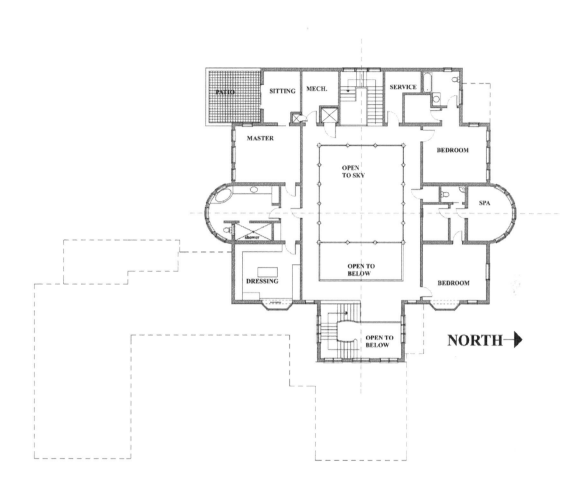

Villa Home – 2nd Floor Plan

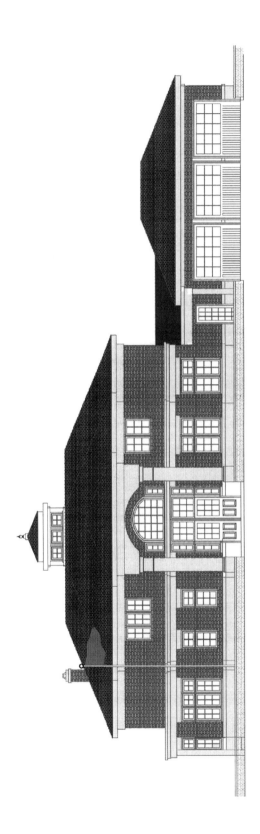

Suburban Home – East Elevation

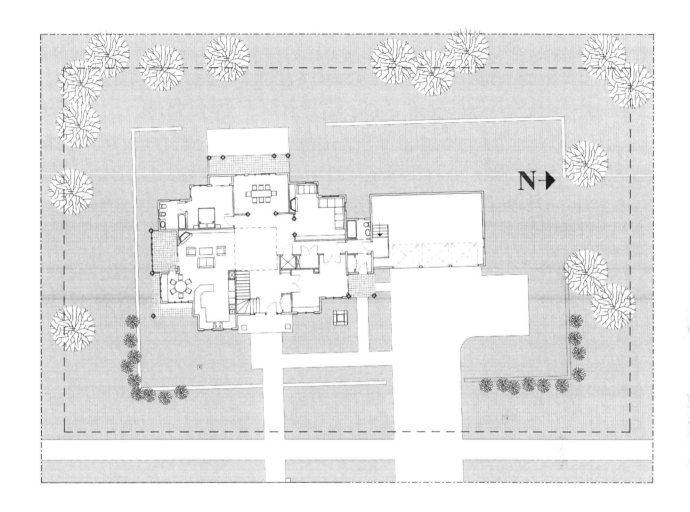

Suburban Home – Site Plan

Afterward

I hope this book has been helpful to the growing numbers of Vastu enthusiasts around the globe. Once again I encourage the reader to work with an experienced Vastu architect in creating a Vastu space. The principles of Vastu science are simple on the whole but require a good amount of experience in application to modern buildings.

I will continue to add educational materials and some Vastu house plans on the website (www. vastu-design.com). Please email me at vastuved@gmail.com if you wish to join our mailing list for new publications and information.

In the coming decades, life on the planet will most likely undergo some big challenges due to the existing trajectories of modern lifestyles and ambitions. I encourage all to re-evaluate their lifestyle and make choices to simplify their life and space in consideration of long term sustainable living for all forms of life on the Earth. In fact, it may be that the time for creating new structures for humans to occupy is coming to an end. New Vastu structures may only be reserved for temples that shine their influence to the surrounding community.

If you are going to create a new Vastu space, please consider your needs carefully and favor simple, smallish structures made of natural, local products. This in itself will be a profound gesture of gratitude to the source and foundation of your Vastu space: Mother Earth.

Bibliography

Temples of Space Science, Dr. V. Ganapati Sthapati

Sthapati's Visit to Mayan Land, Dr. V. Ganapati Sthapati

The Building Architecture of Sthapatya Veda, Dr. V. Ganapati Sthapati

Who Created God, Dr. V. Ganapati Sthapati

Ayadi Calculations, Dr. V. Ganapati Sthapati

Aintiram, Translation by Dr. S. P. Sabarathnam

What is a Temple?, Dr. V. Ganapati Sthapati

Indian Sculpture and Iconography, Dr. V. Ganapati Sthapati

Fabric of the Universe, Dr. Jessie Mercay

Vastu Purusha Mandala, Dr. V. Ganapati Sthapati

The Smile of Murugan, Michael Wood

Index

Indexed by Wendy Stegall - www.Bollywoodiowa.com